A PSYCHOBIOGRAPHY OF
BOBBY FISCHER

A PSYCHOBIOGRAPHY OF BOBBY FISCHER

Understanding the Genius, Mystery, and Psychological Decline of a World Chess Champion

By

JOSEPH G. PONTEROTTO, PH.D.

C H A R L E S   C   T H O M A S • P U B L I S H E R, LTD.
Springfield • Illinois • U.S.A.

Published and Distributed Throughout the World by

CHARLES C THOMAS • PUBLISHER, LTD.
2600 South First Street
Springfield, Illinois 62704

© 2012 by CHARLES C THOMAS • PUBLISHER, LTD.

ISBN 978-0-398-08742-5 (hard)
ISBN 978-0-398-08740-1 (paper)
ISBN 978-0-398-08741-8 (ebook)

Library of Congress Catalog Card Number: 2011051219

With THOMAS BOOKS *careful attention is given to all details of manufacturing
and design. It is the Publisher's desire to present books that are satisfactory as to their
physical qualities and artistic possibilities and appropriate for their particular use.*
THOMAS BOOKS *will be true to those laws of quality that assure a good name
and good will.*

Printed in the United States of America
MM-R-3

PHOTO PERMISSIONS

Front Cover: Bobby Fischer by Hans Namuth, Gelatin Silver Print,
1963, National Portrait Gallery, Smithsonian Institution; gift of the Estate of
HansNamuth, © Hans Namuth Ltd. NPG.95.136, reprinted with permission.

Library of Congress Cataloging-in-Publication Data

Ponterotto, Joseph G.
    A psychobiography of Bobby Fischer : understanding the genius,
mystery, and psychological decline of a world chess champion / by
Joseph G. Ponterotto.
        p. cm.
    Includes bibliographical references and index.
    ISBN 978-0-398-08742-5 (hard) -- ISBN 978-0-398-08740-1 (pbk.)
-- ISBN 978-0-398-08741-8 (ebook)
    1. Fischer, Bobby, 1943–2008–Psychology. 2. Chess players–United
States–Biography. 3. Chess–Psychological aspects. I. Title.

GV1439.F5P66 2012
794.1092–dc23
[B]
                                                        2011051219

Dear Marilee,

Anna talks so highly of you and your work. It is a pleasure to meet you through Anna. I am excited to read your two books that Anna left for me.

In Memory of:

Robert (Bobby) James Fischer (1943–2008)

Dr. Regina (Wender) (Fischer) Pustan (1913–1997)

Joan (Fischer) Targ (1937–1998) and Dr. Elisabeth Targ (1961–2002)

*A family of national and international
historical significance in the twentieth century.*

Good luck with your future plans and best always

Warmly

Ave Parlot

12/17/14

AUTHOR'S NOTE

The Genesis of My Book on Bobby Fischer

I started playing chess in 1972 at the age of 14. Like thousands of American teenagers at the time, the impetus to play chess was an American hero: Bobby Fischer. In the streets of the Bronx where I grew up in the 1960s, the activities year-round were street sports (we had no parks or fields nearby): Stickball and softball in the spring and summer days, and ringalevio (a chase and catch game) at night; touch football, basketball, and roller hockey in the fall and winter; then back to stickball and softball as the spring weather arrived. No one, that I recall, played chess. On a rainy summer day, we might have played monopoly, stratego, battleship, or cards, but the game of chess never entered our discussions. That is, not until the summer of 1972.

Bobby Fischer playing against Boris Spassky was not a game to us, but a war; a war between a lonely, self-assured, cocky, confident, school-disliking (like us) American kid from Brooklyn (although we did not think that highly of Brooklyn in my section of the Bronx) battling all of Russia (I do not think we used the term Soviet Union back then). We were all very competitive, and this chess match, in a place we had never heard of, Reykjavik, Iceland, forced us to learn to play chess so we could follow what was going on in that faraway place we could hardly find on our globe. Thank God for Shelby Lyman and PBS. For the first time in our young lives, my friends and I were actually watching public television, to our parents' astonishment.

After the world championship match in 1972 most of my friends drifted away from chess, especially since Bobby stopped playing competitively—there was no longer our chess hero to follow. I continued playing, however, joining the chess club at Cardinal Spellman High School in the Bronx and playing whenever I could throughout high school and college. Whenever I really wanted to play and there were no same-age peers around, there was always my younger brother John, who though 7 years younger was always brilliant and he picked up the game fairly quickly to the point of providing me good competition. However, he did refuse to read my library chess books I offered him; I could never understand why. John was usually open to a game if I bribed him with a post-game car ride for pizza, carvel ice cream, or Dunkin donuts. Thank you, John!

By my college years in the late 1970s at Iona College in New Rochelle, New York, I was playing chess only infrequently, and by then we had lost total touch with the career and life of Bobby Fischer (this was before the Internet). Chess was never far from my mind though, and whenever I had to present a topic orally in class, I managed to link the class topic (whatever it may have been) to one of my three passions, chess and Bobby Fischer, soccer and Pele, or the red wines of Italy and Northern California (yes, I did manage to graduate). It was also during college where as a psychology major I wrote my first paper on "The Psychology of Chess" for an abnormal psychology class taught by Dr. Paul Greene, a gifted psychologist, teacher, and clinical supervisor. I got an "A" on the paper, which was a bit surprising as I was considered a poor writer. I found out later that Dr. Greene was a chess fan himself and quite a good player. I think that probably helped my grade a bit.

As I got on with my career first as Ph.D. student in Counseling Psychology at the University of California at Santa Barbara, and then as a tenure-track academic researcher at the University of Nebraska-Lincoln and then Fordham University, Lincoln Center Campus, NY, I lost touch with chess. Then in 1992, when Fischer reemerged from his professional and social isolation (in what Brady [2011] and many others have deemed his "wilderness years") for a rematch with Boris Spassky, I got reconnected with the Fischer story. Now, with the internet, it was easy to follow any news on Fischer whether he was in Yugoslavia, Hungary, Japan, the Philippines, Iceland, or elsewhere.

In January of 2008, the week Bobby Fischer passed away, I began writing about his story, not his chess story, but his inner psychology story. This book is the culmination of that research and reflection.

Initially, my intention was to write a scholarly psychological assessment article for a scientific journal, a type of writing and research I was much more familiar with. However, as my work continued and as respected colleagues read early drafts of my psychological assessment of Fischer, a common reaction was that I "should consider writing a book on this topic and reach beyond the scientific community." I thought about this suggestion for a while and realized that if I were to write a book-length psychobiography of Fischer, I would need access to Fischer "intimates," those who knew him very well, as well as access to a full archival base of documents not only on Bobby Fischer, but also on select family members.

With these considerations in mind I set out to have personal contact with three key resources, or Fischer insiders: Dr. Frank Brady, his internationally renowned biographer and former friend (Brady, 1965, 1973, 2011); Russell Targ, Bobby's brother-in-law who was married to Bobby's sister Joan, and who knew Bobby most of his life; and the journalist team of Clea Benson and Peter Nicholas, who were the visionary and groundbreaking investigative journalists who first uncovered, through the Freedom of Information Act, the 900+ page FBI file on Regina Fischer, Bobby's mother. When all three of these resources graciously agreed to talk with me at length, on multiple occasions, I knew that I had a story to tell. I would use my quantitative and qualitative research skills as a multicultural psychologist to delve deeply into Bobby Fischer's life story, and hopefully provide the most comprehensive, in-depth, and balanced psychological profile heretofore published on the country's first official world chess champion.

PREFACE

This book focuses on the inner psychological life of Bobby Fischer in the hopes of gaining a better understanding and deeper insight into his behavior. Among the topics explored are Bobby Fischer's family history, early childhood, development as a chess genius, possible mental illness, and his eerie comparison to the legendary American chess champion, Paul Morphy, who lived and played a century earlier. I also speculate as to how Bobby Fischer's life may have turned out had he received counseling and psychological treatment starting in childhood.

The current text is not meant to be a general biography, as Bobby Fischer has already been the subject of a number of such books. Dr. Frank Brady's *Profile of a Prodigy* (1973) and *Endgame* (2011) top the lists of the most widely acclaimed and read biographies on Fischer, and there are a number of other biographies or detailed accounts of his 1972 world championship victory. This book is a psychobiography that answers many of the psychological questions left unexplored in biographies or documentaries on Bobby Fischer.

The audience for this book includes mental health professionals of varied specialty areas, particularly those interested in working with gifted and talented youth and adolescents, those interested in biographies of puzzling and complex subjects, and individuals interested in chess and chess history. Though a couple of chapters are particularly targeted for mental health professionals, most of the book is written for the layperson without advanced psychological training. The book is organized along ten chapters, and includes various appendices for readers interested in more detail on certain subjects.

Chapter One orients the reader to the nature of psychobiography, to the particular ethical challenges involved in providing a psychological assessment of a recently deceased public figure, and to the particular research methods employed by the author. In Chapter Two, the familiar story of Bobby Fischer's rise to chess supremacy and his decline into possible mental illness is recounted. Bobby's place and ranking among all world chess champions is considered, and a very brief review on the history of chess is provided.

Chapter Three begins the psychological study of Bobby Fischer, starting with a review of his early childhood and living environment. The seeds of Bobby's extraordinary chess ability–visual memory, concentration and focus, spatial relations, original and creative thinking–as well as his psychological problems–awkward social skills, marked distrust, problems academically–become evident in this time period.

A core component in understanding Bobby Fischer is to know his parents, as unraveling the mystery of Bobby Fischer begins with unraveling the perplexity of his ancestry. Who was Regina Wender Fischer? Who was his father? What kind of relationship did Bobby have with his parents, and what was the impact of these relationships on his psychological development? Chapter Four is devoted to understanding Regina Fischer in all her complexity–loving, but overwhelmed single mother, a social justice and peace activist, and a multilingual scholar who would earn, in time, both M.D. and Ph.D. degrees. Critical to understanding Regina Fischer's life is consideration of the context of the Cold War period and the fact that she was under FBI investigation as a possible Soviet spy. This chapter integrates a 994-page FBI file on Regina (Wender) Fischer, which the author acquired through the Freedom of Information Act.

Gerhardt (Liebscher) Fischer, born in 1908 in Berlin, Germany, is listed on Bobby Fischer's 1943 birth certificate as the father. The majority of Bobby Fischer researchers, however, including this author, is fairly convinced that Dr. Paul Felix Nemenyi, a Hungarian-born American scientist, was Bobby Fischer's biological father. Chapter Five systematically examines the evidence regarding Bobby's paternity. The lack of a stable, reliable father-son relationship for a psychologically vulnerable young Bobby Fischer would have a lasting impact on his personality development and mental health over time.

In Chapter Six, the psychological development of Bobby Fischer is examined more closely. Building off of the previous three chapters, this chapter explores possible rationales for Bobby Fischer's intense feelings of anger and mistrust, and hypothesizes why a primary outlet of his anger was towards Jews. This chapter sets the stage for a more systematic and detailed assessment of Bobby's mental state.

A formal post-mortem psychological assessment, a "psychological autopsy," is the focus of Chapter Seven. The rationale for such an assessment in terms of informing the mental health field is highlighted. Perhaps the most technical and clinically detailed section in the book, this chapter reviews available observational evidence on different mental disorders that have been associated with Bobby Fischer in previous literature. Ultimately, the chapter presents a differential diagnosis of Bobby Fischer and hypotheses what mental illness he may have had.

Readers knowledgeable of chess history specifically, or American history of the mid-nineteenth century, generally, will know the name of Paul Morphy. An international chess phenomenon born in New Orleans, Morphy captivated America and the world with his chess feats and victories in the late 1850s. In fact, the excitement and uproar created by Morphy resembles that resulting from Bobby's 1972 world championship victory over a century later. Though there have been many great American chess champions in the last two centuries, none have had the impact, nor held the legendary status, of Morphy and Fischer. Sadly, Morphy, like Fischer, appeared to succumb to increasing states of paranoia and mental illness. This chapter compares the lives and psychologies of these two great American chess champions.

Paul Morphy and Bobby Fischer were not the only chess grandmasters to be associated with mental illness. What is it about chess genius and mental illness? Are the two linked in some way? Chapter Nine reviews the history of mental illness among great chess players and integrates the empirical research on any possible linkage between states of originality/creativity (common to elite chess skill) and mental illness.

Finally, Chapter Ten outlines possible psychological supports and treatments that may have helped Bobby Fischer (and family members) at various points in his development. This chapter explores the following questions: If Bobby would have received psychological counseling beginning in early childhood, would his life had turned out differently? Could psychological treatment have distracted Bobby from his passion and obsession for chess, thus hindering his opportunity to reach the world title? Or could psychological treatment have equipped him with the psychological resources and coping skills that would have facilitated not only his reaching the world chess championship, but also a more balanced and stable personal, family, and professional life? The chapter also includes suggestions for early school and family intervention and psychoeducation regarding the needs and challenges of the gifted and talented. I invite the reader on this journey of exploration and insight into the psychological character of Bobby Fischer.

J.G.P.

ACKNOWLEDGMENTS

PRIMARY SOURCES OF SUPPORT AND ENCOURAGEMENT

A Psychobiography of Bobby Fischer represents my thirteenth authored or edited book, yet by far my most challenging effort, and the one where I was most dependent on the assistance, generosity, wisdom, and experiences of others to bring my vision of Bobby Fischer's psychological history to life. The first person I thank and acknowledge is Russell Targ, Bobby Fischer's brother-in-law. Mr. Targ met Bobby when he was, in his own words, "courting his sister, Joan" (Targ, 2008, p. 237). Bobby was 14 years old at the time. I venture that there is no person alive who knew Bobby better than Russell Targ. Mr. Targ is a world-renowned researcher on remote viewing and the author of at least eight books, including his riveting and revealing autobiography titled, *Do You See what I see? Memoirs of a Blind Biker: Lasers and Love, ESP and the CIA, and the Meaning of Life* (Targ, 2008). Mr. Targ, who is now 78 years old, continues to conduct research and travels to train others in distance healing practices. During the time we were in some regular contact, Mr. Targ was first off to Paris, France to accept a Life Achievement Award from the International Association of Parapsychology, and then off to New Zealand to conduct remote viewing research.

I had the honor of three long phone interviews with Mr. Targ as well as numerous back-and-forth e-mails to clarify questions as well as to get his reaction to my earlier (Ponterotto, 2011) writing on his brother-in-law Bobby. Furthermore, Mr. Targ read and commented on earlier versions of Chapters Four and Five of this book focusing on profiles of Bobby's mother Regina Fischer, and his likely biological father Paul Nemenyi. Mr. Targ also granted me permission to use photos from his family archive. Without Russell Targ's support for this project (not that he agrees with all of my conclusions) and his insights on the Fischer family, this book may not have been possible.

The second person who encouraged and empowered me to keep studying and working on the life of Bobby Fischer was the esteemed and internationally renowned biographer, Dr. Frank Brady, of nearby (to me at Fordham University) St. John's University in Queens, New York. When I first contacted Dr. Brady in the summer of 2010, he was finishing up, unbeknownst to me, work on his latest biography of Fischer titled *Endgame: Bobby Fischer's Remarkable Rise and Fall–from America's Brightest Prodigy to the Edge of Madness* (Brady, 2011). As busy as Dr. Brady was with proofing galley pages, securing photo permissions, planning the release of his book, all the while being a full-time professor preparing for fall classes and finishing up summer administrative work (he had just stepped down from serving as Chair of the Mass Communications Department at St. John's University), he made time to meet with me multiple times in person, and helped me repeatedly through e-mail correspondence. In addition to his three biographies of Bobby Fischer, Dr. Brady has published highly successful and acclaimed biographies of Orson Wells, Aristotle Onassis, Hugh Heffner, and Barbara Streisand. Though I am not a biographer by training, I believe it fair to credit Dr. Frank Brady as one of the most important and impactful biographers of the last half-century.

While I consider Mr. Russell Targ my Fischer family member mentor, I consider Dr. Brady my mentor in the field of biography. At one lecture Dr. Brady gave at the Marshall Chess Club (where he is current President) in New York City after the release of *Endgame* in February, 2011, he advised those in the audience interested in biography to "read everything there is on your subject, interview everyone you can who knew him or her; even if you do not use all the information, at least you are coming from a place of knowledge and competence." Though my own biographical research experience pales in comparison to Dr. Brady's, I have tried my best to live up to his advice.

A third trove of information and insights on Bobby Fischer and his life was provided to me by Dr. Anthony Saidy, a medical doctor, an International Chess Master, and a one-time close friend of Bobby Fischer. Dr. Saidy is a leading chess author, and two of his books, *The March of Chess Ideas* (Saidy, 1994) and *The World of Chess* (Saidy & Lessing, 1974), can be considered classics in the field. Dr. Saidy was the Canadian Open Chess Co-Champion in 1960, the American Open Chess Championship in 1967 and Co-Champion in 1992, the U.S. Speed Champion in 1956, and he placed fourth in the 1974 U.S. Chess Championship (behind Walter Browne, Pal Benko, and Larry Evans). At his peak playing strength around 1964, Dr. Saidy's ELO rating was 2532.

In any in-depth review of Bobby Fischer's chess career and personal life, Dr. Saidy figures prominently. For example, in Brad Darrach's (2009) controversial book, *Bobby Fischer vs. the Rest of the World,* Dr. Saidy is portrayed as the key person in helping Bobby actually get to Reykjavik, Iceland for the 1972 World Chess Championship match. Dr. Saidy shared with me that

Darrach's portrayal of him and the circumstances leading up to Bobby's trip to Iceland was 80 percent accurate (and 20% fabricated). It is fair to say, that without Dr. Saidy's friendship, patience, ingenuity, and support, Bobby Fischer would have never made the trip to Reykjavik for his 1972 match against Boris Spassky. Dr. Saidy is featured in two documentaries on Bobby, "Anything to Win: The Genius and Madness of Bobby Fischer" (2004) and the more recently released "Bobby Fischer Against the World" (2011). In these documentaries, Dr. Saidy's passion for the game of chess, and his admiration for and appreciation of Bobby's accomplishments on the chessboard, are touchingly evident.

Dr. Saidy read my 2011 *Miller-McCune Magazine* article on Bobby Fischer (Ponterotto, 2011) and offered insights, reflections, and memories on his time with Bobby that substantially extended the personal depth of my understanding of Bobby and his family. Furthermore, Dr. Saidy read, commented on, and in fact helped copy-edit (he is a gifted editor as well as author) this entire book. He also provided me with valuable leads for areas to pursue in my study of Bobby Fischer, his mother Regina and grandmother Natalie Wender, and the political context of the times. I feel deeply indebted to Dr. Saidy for his careful reading of this entire book, for his professional guidance and insights, and for his humor, good nature, and personal support.

My fourth source of support, and perhaps the greatest in terms of the sheer volume of information and the amount of time they provided me, was the journalism team of Clea Benson and Peter Nicholas. While working for the *Philadelphia Inquirer* in the early 2000s, Nicholas and Benson discovered and secured, through the Freedom of Information Act, a 900-page FBI dossier on Regina Fischer. They subsequently requested and received the FBI files of Regina's husband (married from 1933 until her 1945 divorce), Hans Gerhardt Fischer. As I read more of this team's work, as well as began to understand more fully the thoroughness and completeness of their inquiry methods (extensive interviews conducted internationally, archival document discovery across multiple languages, rigorous convergent validity methods in assessing data accuracy), it began to dawn on me that their investigative work was raising the status of research on Bobby Fischer and his family to a new plateau of scholarly sophistication. Benson and Nicholas's decade-long research program (along with Dr. Brady's almost 50 years of research on Bobby) has provided a springboard for more recent researchers, including myself, Edmonds and Eidinow (2004), among others to further extend the research on Bobby Fischer, one of the most interesting and enigmatic celebrities and intellectuals of the last half-century. By the empirical research standards of any scientific profession, the work and contributions of Benson and Nicholas have been groundbreaking.

As I was somewhat new to biographical methods at the start of this Fischer project, I was also new to the field of journalism, and had much to learn. Benson and Nicholas, particularly Clea Benson who organizes, logs, and maintains the team's Fischer archives, taught me much of what I now know of investigative journalism.

A fifth primary source of information on Bobby Fischer and his family was Dr. Robert Lipton, who now serves as an Associate Professor in the Department of Emergency Medicine at the University of Michigan. Dr. Lipton had kindly e-mailed me to offer family insights after reading my article on Bobby Fischer that appeared in *Miller-McCune Magazine* (Ponterotto, 2011). Dr. Lipton met and dated Elisabeth Targ, Bobby Fischer's niece, while Elisabeth was completing her psychiatry residency at the University of California at Los Angeles in the late 1980s. Dr. Lipton got to know the Fischer family well, particularly Elisabeth's mom [who was Bobby's older sister], Joan Fischer Targ; in fact he remarked to me that Joan "was effectively my surrogate mother" (R. Lipton, personal communication, January 28, 2011). Dr. Lipton and Elisabeth eventually separated as boyfriend-girlfriend, but the two remained close friends until Elisabeth's untimely death in 2002 at the age of 40 (see Targ, 2008). Given Elisabeth was living in Santa Monica while she was at UCLA, and Bobby was living in the area as well, some of the responsibility in caring for and helping Bobby and at times his mother Regina, fell on Elisabeth and Robert.

Dr. Lipton's insights are particularly insightful for four reasons. First, he was very close to Elisabeth and her family, particularly Joan Fischer. Second, he helped Bobby during his "wilderness years" where we have little validated information about Bobby's life. Third, both he and Elisabeth were in the mental health research field–Elisabeth an M.D. Psychiatrist, and Robert a Ph.D. in Psychiatric Epidemiology (with a minor in psychocultural anthropology)–and thus their clinical insights, which Dr. Lipton shared with me, have important value in our understanding of the psychological life of Bobby Fischer. Fourth, Robert spent time with Regina Fischer in her later years and his observations of Regina and her life with her children/grandchildren is particularly important because much of the literature on Regina Fischer stems from earlier stages in her life (e.g., as in the FBI reports which spanned 1942 to 1973, and memories of the chess community in the 1950s and 1960s). Dr. Lipton was also kind enough to read and comment on Chapter Four of this book, "Mother Love: Understanding Regina Fischer's Relationship with son Bobby."

Additional Sources of Consultation and Support

Without the support and encouragement of Russell Targ and Dr. Frank Brady, likely the two persons alive who knew Bobby Fischer best, I don't know if I would have felt that I even had the right to pen a psychological life story of Mr. Fischer. And without the support and mentoring of journalists Clea Benson and Peter Nicholas, the assistance of Fischer family friend, Dr. Robert Lipton, and the insights of Fischer close friend Dr. Anthony Saidy, this book would not be the integrative vision and window into Bobby Fischer's life that I think it has become. However, there were many other colleagues, professionals, and Fischer associates who provided me with valuable assistance over the last four years as I researched and wrote this book.

First, I thank my wife and colleague, Dr. Ingrid Grieger, a master clinician and clinical supervisor, who not only read earlier versions of this work, but also helped me understand and process early childhood aspects of Bobby Fischer's life that would relate to his long-term psychological development. Interestingly, Ingrid and family moved to the Eastern Parkway section of Brooklyn, around the block from Bobby Fischer's family (who were at 560 Lincoln Place) in 1954, and Ingrid remembers seeing Bobby in the neighborhood. Dr. Grieger's expertise in understanding Jewish immigrants, particularly those associated with the Holocaust, was very valuable to my understanding of the Fischer family sociocultural-religious context in the 1940s and 1950s.

Other colleagues who are experienced psychologists (some are also chess players) that read and commented on early versions of this work include Dr. Paul Greene (whom I mention in the book Preface) of Iona College, Drs. Amelio D'Onofrio and Daniel Ruckdeschel of Fordham University, and Dr. Rahul Chauhan, in private practice in New York City. All experienced clinicians, representing diverse psychotherapeutic orientations–humanistic, existential, family systems, cognitive-behavioral, psychodynamic, and multicultural–these scholars helped me understand more fully, and interpret more clearly, the complexity of Bobby Fischer's psychological life. Furthermore, these psychologists consulted with me on the ethical appropriateness of my psychological assessment and profile of Bobby Fischer and his mother Regina Fischer.

Other mental health, medical, or legal experts who consulted with me on the ethical issues involved in this psychobiography were Drs. Doyle McCarthy and Akane Zusho of Fordham University's Institutional Review Board (IRB), Drs. Stephen Behnke and Lindsay Childress-Beatty of the American Psychological Association, Dr. Celia Fisher of Fordham University's Center for Ethics Education, Dr. Marcus Zachary at Saint Francis hospital in San

Francisco, and Joel Silverman, Esq., in New York City. I say more about my ethics consultation with these professionals in Chapter One.

A chess insider who was very helpful to my research was Paul M. Albert, Jr. Mr. Albert is a serious player and lover of chess, a successful investment banker, investor, and corporate director and the former well-known sponsor of the "Albert Brilliancy Prizes" from 1983 to 2003 awarded to the competitors in the U.S. Chess Championship who played the most brilliant and innovative games at the tournament. Mr. Albert was also a trustee of the American Chess Foundation from 1970s until 2003 (see Albert, 2004) and provided me with a penetrating window into chess life and politics during that era. Mr. Albert also met Bobby Fischer on several occasions and handled the demonstration board for a few games at the Marshall Chess Club in 1965 when Bobby was playing via teletype (he could not receive State Department permission to travel to Cuba) in the Capablanca Memorial Tournament held in Havana (Albert, 2009). Given the esteem and respect in which Mr. Albert is held in the U.S. chess world, his kind introductions allowed me access to other chess notables in Bobby Fischer's era. Particularly, through Mr. Albert's introduction I met and spent time with Grandmaster William Lombardy, who of course figured so prominently in Bobby Fischer's rise to the World Chess title. I thank Paul Albert for his generous time, insight, memories and guidance.

A helpful source of information on the life and personality of Bobby Fischer was Shernaz Kennedy, an International Woman's Master who was a friend and confidant of Bobby's for roughly two decades, from 1981 through 2001. Shernaz and Bobby maintained a close relationship through regular mail correspondence and phone calls. Furthermore, Shernaz visited Bobby for four days in Los Angeles in 1986. Bobby appeared to trust Shernaz and he shared with her his thoughts and feelings on many personal, family, and professional topics. Shernaz, in turn, was and is very loyal to Bobby and I feel fortunate to have had the opportunity to communicate with Shernaz through long phone conversations and multiple e-mails. I also thank Grandmaster William Lombardy for the enlightening dinner and lunch conversations we had regarding his life and his relationship with Bobby Fischer.

I am indebted to Dr. Thomas Aiello, professor of history at Valdosta State University, and one of the country's leading experts on the life and times of chess legend Paul Morphy. Professor Aiello reviewed an earlier version of Chapter Eight on the parallel lives of Bobby Fischer and Paul Morphy and made valuable suggestions that helped me to enhance the clarity and accuracy of the chapter. Dr. Aiello's knowledge of Paul Morphy, of Morphy's chief biographer, David Lawson, and of life in the South (particularly New Orleans) in the mid-nineteenth century is astonishing. An eminent author and editor, Dr. Aiello's recent books include *Dan Burley's Jive* (2009), *The Kings of Casino Park: Race and Race Baseball in the Lost Season of 1932* (2011), and *Bayou Classic: The Grambling-Southern Football Rivalry* (2011). Thank you Dr. Aiello for your thoughtful review and comments.

I also want to acknowledge and thank Dr. William Todd Schultz of Pacific University in Oregon, one of our nation's eminent psychobiographers. Prior to beginning my research on Bobby Fischer I did not know Dr. Shultz personally, but nonetheless when I contacted him he graciously offered me his advice and recommendations, and led me to definitive sources and exemplar models of psychobiography. Dr. Schultz, in his own work, highlights that good psychobiography is not "pathography," that is, the reduction of a complex personality to static psychopathological categories or symptoms. He emphasized that it is critical for the psychobiographer to capture the essence of the subject's thoughts and feelings that underlie the behavior we witness. Dr. Schultz read an earlier brief manuscript on Bobby Fischer and provided me with valuable assistance and constructive criticism. Dr. Schultz's (2011) newest psychobiography was recently released by Oxford University Press: *Tiny Terror: Why Truman Capote (Almost) Wrote Answered Prayers.*

Other individuals who contributed to this book in some way included Dr. Diane Ponterotto, a feminist-oriented psycholinguist at the University of Rome (Italy) who helped me monitor any potential bias as a man writing about the women in Bobby Fischer's life, particularly his mother, Regina Fischer, and his sister Joan Fischer. Dr. Richard Ross, of New York City, a close acquaintance of the chess legend and psychoanalyst Dr. Reuben Fine in his later years, provided me with valuable insights into the personality and character of this historic figure in chess history. Salvatore Franco of Minneapolis, Minnesota expended strong effort in helping me try to locate a former Fischer acquaintance. Albert Audette, a retired Air Force colonel, and now head of Audette & Associates, LLC, helped me understand the relationship between the FBI and the military in the 1960s. Dalia Wissgott-Moneta, a social worker in Frankfurt, Germany, and Professors Susan Ray and Suzanne Hafner of Fordham University, assisted me with translation of German documents. A few of our Fordham University Ph.D. students were helpful in terms of discussions we had related to the Bobby Fischer story, particularly Alex Fietzer, Esther Fingerhut, and Jason Reynolds.

I acknowledge the generosity of Einar Einarsson and Svala Soleyg, friends of Bobby Fischer's in Iceland who granted me permission to reproduce their "last" photo and pencil drawing of Bobby Fischer. Thanks as well to Dr. Alfredo Pasin of Monza, Italy, for allowing me to reproduce his poem "Il Giocatore Bobby" ("Bobby the Chess Player") in its entirety in this volume.

Finally, I acknowledge the assistance of the Federal Bureau of Investigation (FBI) who honored my Freedom of Information Act (FOIA) request for all documents pertaining to Bobby Fischer's mother, Regina (Wender) Fischer (Pustan). Knowing the length of Regina's file and the many requests the FBI Records Management Division likely receives on a weekly basis, I anticipated a long, drawn-out process in securing all relevant files. However, FBI staff responded immediately to my requests and was very helpful. I am particularly indebted to David M. Hardy, Section Chief, and David P. Sobonya, Public Information Officer and Legal Administrative Specialist, of the Record/Information Dissemination Section of the FBI. Furthermore, I acknowledge the assistance of Linda Wilkins, Public Affairs Specialist, and Susan McKee, Unit Chief, Investigative Publicity and Public Affairs Unit, Office of Public Affairs, for their assistance in helping me secure FBI permission to reproduce the photo of a young Regina Wender that appeared in the FBI documents.

CONTENTS

LIST OF ILLUSTRATIONS

PRAISE FOR

A Psychobiography of Bobby Fischer:
Understanding the Genius, Mystery, and Psychological Decline
of a World Chess Champion

"The era of the amateur psychologizing about Bobby Fischer is coming to a close. Now we heed a professional. Dr. Joseph Ponterotto has applied the scientific principles of his discipline to a personality that so long perplexed the world. The controversies will not end, but any further hypotheses will need to take Ponterotto's work as a starting point."
 –Anthony Saidy, MD., Intl. Chess Master

"Dr. Ponterotto's pioneering research on Bobby Fischer clears up many of the myths and misperceptions that have long surrounded one of the world's most enigmatic personalities. This book is a unique blend of psychology and reporting that will fascinate anyone who has ever wondered what explains such self-destructive brilliance."
 –Clea Benson and Peter Nicholas, Investigative Journalists

"Brilliant, agonized; original, immature; astute, emotionally volatile; virtuosic, enigmatic–so goes the narrative of the life and adventures of Bobby Fischer, a man who captivated the world with both his genius and with his tormented soul. In *A Psychobiography of Bobby Fischer,* Joseph Ponterotto elegantly unpacks the many contradictions that at once propelled Fischer onto the world stage and, at the same time, led to his eventual liminalization. Ponterotto traces Fischer's socioemotional development from early life skillfully integrating the many influences that helped shape the person he became as an adult. His treatment of the tumultuous dynamics of Fischer's relationship with his mother and the psychological implications of the mystery of his paternity not only makes for fascinating reading but poignantly sheds light on what Fischer's hidden suffering was all about. While Ponterotto explores Fischer's life with the eye of a scientist, he writes with the pen of one who appreciates the complexity of human experience and who faithfully and compassionately strives to follow the truth wherever it may lead. I recommend this eminently readable work not only to Bobby Fischer fans but to all those fascinated by the paradoxes and pain that often lie behind genius."

   −Amelio A. D'Onofrio, Ph.D.
      Founding Director and Clinical Professor
      Psychological Services Institute, Fordham University

"The link between genius and mental illness is often observed but rarely resolved. Chess genius Bobby Fischer's oddities give way to accomplished academician and chess lover Joseph Ponterotto's systematic application of contemporary psychology. Dr. Ponterotto shows us greater meaning in the tragic life of one of the superstars of modern chess. Had proper help been available to a young Bobby Fischer, what elegance of chess mastery might the world have experienced? What discoveries do we lose today when families and children don't get the best support and fall into the abyss of mental illness? Dr. Ponterotto has uncovered the moves and mistakes in one troubled genius to show us how we can help people play the game of life so that there are more winners, and amazingly, fewer losers."

   −Paul Greene, Ph.D.
      Professor of Psychology, Iona College, New Rochelle, NY
      Private Practice, New York City and New Rochelle, NY

"In reading this psychobiography of Bobby Fischer, I felt as if I was invited along on an intriguing journey to explore both his genius at the board, and his inexplicable behavior off the board. I have come to understand the complex intermix of factors−historical, cultural, political, genetic, personal, and family−that contributed to Mr. Fischer's development in both healthy and unhealthy ways. Professor Ponterotto anchors his discussion and conclusions in serious scholarship while writing about Bobby Fischer and his family in an accessible and respectful manner. I highly recommend taking this journey into the mind of perhaps history's greatest chess legend."

   −Rahul Chauhan, Ph.D.
      Psychologist and Multicultural Specialist
      Private Practice, New York City

"I was quickly captivated by Dr. Ponterotto's clear, conversational style of writing which made chess and Bobby Fischer both accessible and interesting to me. I learned about the genre of psychobiography and the goals of a psychological autopsy. As a psychologist (and ethics educator) I was gratifed that Ponterotto was deliberate and transparent in his consideration of the ethical issues and limitations involved with this undertaking, and I appreciated that he frequently reminded the reader about the speculative nature of the diagnostic conclusions he was drawing. Mental health professionals will appreciate the story of Fischer's inner life that Ponterotto weaves. It is an intriguing journey to attempt to put together the puzzle (with missing pieces) of Fischer's life, from a psychological perspective. Figuring out "how someone got this way" is at the heart of the diagnostic and assessment process and is difficult enough when the subject is a living active participant. The painstaking research, the multiple interviews, the triangulation of sources, making explicit his thought processes all serve to increase the reader's confidence in Ponterotto's conclusions. (The level of detail in Chapters 4 and 5 on Fischer's mother and likely paternity are good examples of this rigorous research.) It is apparent in Chapters 7 and 9 that Ponterotto is a conscientious scientist and insightful practitioner who applied his ample skills as both a psychological researcher and psychotherapist to unravel the mystery of Bobby Fischer. Ponterotto has made a significant contribution to the scholarship on Bobby Fischer by adding psychology's voice to the speculations about the mental health of this troubled champion.

    –Suzette L. Speight, Ph.D.
      Department of Psychology
      University of Akron, Akron, Ohio

"Through his in-depth study of Bobby Fischer, Dr. Ponterotto provides a riveting case study that can serve as an educative tool for school-based mental health professionals and administrators. Bobby Fischer was a genius, but also deeply troubled; and as highlighted in this psychobiography, early intervention by school counselors and school psychologists may have helped young Bobby both develop his cognitive and intellectual gifts while at the same time promoting his broader academic and social skills development. This book was a fascinating read, and so relevant to the work I do in schools and in private practice. I recommend it highly."

    –Ernest A. Collabolletta, Psy.D.
      School Psychologist, Scarsdale Public Schools,
      and Private Practice, White Plains, NY

"Ponterotto has given us a unique gift: something fundamentally NEW about

Bobby Fischer. His psychobiography doesn't walk the boards paced by count-
less others before him, seeking to score academic points by picking the nits
of place, time, and motive. It isn't a work of sympathy or damnation. Instead,
A Psychobiography of Bobby Fischer provides a considered psychological portrait
of an American enigma and a necessary companion to previous traditional
biographies."
   –Thomas Aiello, Ph.D.
      Assistant Professor of History
      Valdosta State University, Valdosta, GA
      Editor, David Lawson's *Paul Morphy: The Pride and Sorrow of Chess*

"*A Psychobiography of Bobby Fischer* provides a fascinating layer of information
to help interpret the complex and, in some ways, tragic life of Bobby and his
family."
   –Robert Lipton, Ph.D.
      Associate Professor, Department of Emergency Medicine
      University of Michigan, Ann Arbor, MI

A PSYCHOBIOGRAPHY OF
BOBBY FISCHER

Chapter One

BRIEF NOTES ON PSYCHOBIOGRAPHY, PROFESSIONAL ETHICS, AND RESEARCH METHODS

All I want to do, ever, is play chess.
(Bobby Fischer, quoted in Rothstein, 2008, p. B1)

I wish I could fly, so that I could play chess with God.
(Nine-year-old chess player Adam Weser,
cited in Hoffman, 2007, p. 63)

ON THE NATURE OF PSYCHOBIOGRAPHY

Though much has been written about Bobby Fischer, first as a visionary chess genius, and second, as a troubled man who lost his way and became obsessed with Anti-Semitic and Anti-American viewpoints, little is known of the inner workings of his mind that led to the "Mystery of Bobby Fischer." This book attempts to unveil that mystery using the research tools of psychobiography. Put simply, psychobiography is the psychological study of an individual person (Schultz, 2005b). The specialty and research methods of psychobiography are well established in the broader field of psychology and there are numerous models and guides to conducting and reporting exemplar psychobiographical studies (e.g., see Elms, 1994; Runyan, 1982; Schultz, 2005a).

More than a biographical sketch of "who" a person was and "what" the person accomplished in their particular field, psychobiography concerns itself with the "why" of a person's behavior. What was the inner life, the psychology that drove the person to his or her thoughts, feelings, and actions? What were the underlying mechanisms that made the person tick? In this book, I provide one window into the life of Bobby Fischer by using my lens as an academic researcher and practicing psychologist to explore the inner psychology of this legendary and enigmatic icon.

An individual's behavior should be considered within the context of their time–the political and historical period of their lives, their genetic predispositions, the family's immigration and migration history, religious and cultural experiences and influences, socioeconomic conditions, academic experiences, the specific characteristics of the career in which they engage, and their significant friendships and relationships at critical points in development. A comprehensive psychobiography should address all of these facets of an individual life.

In his edited *Handbook of Psychobiography*, Schultz (2005b) outlined the characteristics of quality psychobiographies. First, they are persuasive in that the reader follows the researcher's logic and methods, understands the conclusions made, and finds the interpretations and explanations offered to be credible and accurate given the data reviewed. Second, the "story" is logically laid out, with conclusions and interpretations following the presentation and evaluation of the evidence. Third, comprehensive treatment of the person and the context of the person's life enhances the credibility of the psychobiography. There may be multiple interpretations of a single event, and they all should be explored and then examined in relation to other events to identify common threads of behavior or thought.

A fourth characteristic of good psychobiography emphasized by Schultz (2005b) is what he called "convergence of data" (p. 7). Multiple sources of information relating to the same event enhance the accuracy of interpretation. For example, Regina Fischer, Bobby's mother, figured very prominently in his life. One source of information on Regina Fischer is a 994-page FBI dossier on her. If one were to base her or his opinion only on this source, a narrow (and more negative) picture of Regina and her parenting skills would emerge. However, if one were to "triangulate" the FBI data with perceptions of Regina held by her family (e.g., her son Bobby, her daughter Joan, and her son-in-law Russell Targ), and her friends, a more balanced, and likely accurate picture on Regina Fischer and the nature of her relationship to son Bobby would emerge.

Schultz's (2005b) fifth characteristic of good psychobiography is elucidation and sudden coherence. With careful interpretation based on multiple data sources, what may have been previously confusing or incoherent now makes sense when contextualized within a deeper understanding of the subject. With regard to Bobby Fischer, one might ask what led to his obsessive hatred of two particular segments of the population: first, Jews, and second, the United States government? A coherent and comprehensive psychobiography ultimately arrives at a reasonable answer to this question.

A sixth aspect of a quality psychobiography is that the argument presented throughout is logical and sound, and free from researcher self-contradictions. Seventh, interpretations within psychobiography should be consistent with broader knowledge of human development, cultural expectations, and the specific career in question. Finally, sound psychobiography withstands the test of time and remains a viable explanation for an individual's actions even as other interpretations are introduced (Runyan, 2005; Schultz, 2005b).

In this psychobiography of Bobby Fischer I have strived to meet the first seven criteria for strong biographical research and reporting outlined by Schultz (2005b). The final criteria, credibility of my explanations over time, will be judged in the years to come. I leave it to my readers to weigh the value, validity, and impact of this psychobiography on Bobby Fischer.

ON THE PLACE OF PSYCHOLOGICAL THEORY IN PSYCHOBIOGRAPHY

Psychobiographies can be anchored in a single theory, in multiple theories, or in no theory in particular. For example, both Dr. Ernest Jones's (1951) analysis of Paul Morphy and Reuben Fine's (2008) analysis of Bobby Fischer are exclusively anchored in Freudian psychoanalytic theory. By contrast, Todd Schultz's (2011) recent psychobiography of Truman Capote is anchored in attachment theory and script theory. My view is that to view a historic figure within the lens of one theoretical model is potentially very limiting. Jones's psychoanalytic treatment of Morphy was harshly criticized (e.g., Lawson, 2010; Philipson, 1989) as was Fine's Freudian analysis of Fischer (e.g., Saidy, 2008). In some ways, these psychobiographies fell short on Schultz's (2005b) final criteria of holding up and maintaining interpretive credibility over time and in the eyes of newer scholars. I believe the limits of the one-theory model attenuated the impact and widespread acceptance of the work of Jones and Fine, and perhaps justifiably so.

As a research psychologist and practicing clinician, my day-to-day work is influenced by multiple theoretical models, and I instinctively operated from these multiple models in my effort to understand the inner psychological life of Bobby Fischer. Of particular value to me in studying the life of Bobby Fischer was: (1) the diathesis stress model that looks at the interaction of biological dispositions and environmental circumstances that lead to both the development of psychological strengths and challenges; (2) psychodynamic theory that highlights the importance of early life experiences and adult attachments during childhood; (3) family systems theory that looks at Bobby's life in the context of family dynamics; (4) psychosocial development theory that focuses on critical life tasks over the lifespan; and (5) multicultural theory that incorporates cultural and socioeconomic context in lifestory analysis. I discuss aspects of these theories in various parts of this book.

ETHICAL CONSIDERATIONS

Writing a psychological focused life story of an individual recently deceased is a sensitive task. On one hand I wanted to honor and respect Bobby Fischer's memory and legacy, being fully aware that he is survived by his brother-in-law, two nephews, and great nieces/nephew who may one day read this book (see Targ, 2008). On the other hand, as a psychological researcher, I needed to maintain objectivity in understanding the inner life of Bobby Fischer, including both psychological strengths and challenges. To understand Bobby as fully as a biographer who did not know him can, necessitates deep study of the individual's life, as well as his genetic and family history. This is a deeply personal venture and throughout my work on this book over the past four years I never lost site that I must write in a scholarly, yet respectful, thoughtful, sensitive, and balanced manner.

A particularly sensitive task in writing this psychobiography was addressing the possibility that Bobby Fischer was at some point, mentally ill. If Bobby did suffer from a mental illness recognized in the *Diagnostic and Statistical Manual of Mental Disorders* (American Psychiatric Association, 2000) it is one important aspect of a comprehensive understanding of his life. Though some psychobiographers (e.g., Schultz, 2005b) refrain from hypothesizing specific psychological disorders, my view is that at times such an analysis can add to the comprehensive nature of a life story. In Bobby Fischer's case, accurately understanding his mental states over time could help explain in a more coherent way, behavior that may seem bizarre to the layperson's eye.

Generally speaking, psychologists, mental health counselors, and other mental health professionals (psychiatrists, social workers) do not proffer psychological diagnoses of individuals with whom they have never met and interviewed at length in person. I had never met Bobby Fischer and he certainly was not a patient/client of mine. However, in this book I do explore the topic of mental illness over the course of Bobby's life, and I provide a tentative differential diagnosis. As a psychologist and mental health counselor I am guided by the professional ethical codes of my profession. More specifically, below I quote sections of the ethical codes of both the American Psychological Association (APA) and the American Mental Health Counselors' Association (AMHCA) that relate to my psychological assessment and diagnosis of Bobby Fischer (see Chapter Seven).

From the Code of Ethics of the American Psychological Association (APA)

> Psychologists provide opinions of the psychological characteristics of individuals only after they have conducted an examination of the individual adequate to support their statements or conclusions. When, despite reasonable efforts, such an examination is not practical, psychologists document the efforts they made and the result of those efforts, clarify the probable impact of their limited information on the reliability and validity of their opinions, and appropriately limit the nature and extent of their conclusions or recommendations. (APA, 2002, 9.01(b) Bases for Assessment, p. 13)

From the Code of Ethics of the American Mental Health Counselors' Association (AMHCA)

    a. Mental health counselors base their diagnoses and other assessment summaries on multiple sources of data whenever possible.

    b. Mental health counselors are careful not to draw conclusions unless empirical evidence is present.

    c. Mental health counselors consider multicultural factors (including but not limited to gender, race, religion, age, ability, culture, class, ethnicity, sexual orientation) in test interpretation, in diagnosis, and in the formulation of prognosis and treatment recommendations.

    f. Mental health counselors write reports in a style that is clear, concise and easily accessible to the lay reader. (AMHCA, 2010, Section 1, D [Assessment and Diagnosis], code 2 [Interpretation and Reporting], a, b, c, and f, pp. 10–11)

In this book I weigh available observational evidence for various mental illnesses that have been attributed to Bobby Fischer in the literature and media. Various authors have hypothesized that Bobby might have suffered from Asperger's Disorder, Paranoid Schizophrenia, Paranoid Personality Disorder, Delusional Disorder, among others (see Chapter Seven). Though I do hypothesize that Bobby Fischer likely suffered from mental illness at certain points in his life, I emphasize at the outset that the diagnoses are only speculative in that Bobby Fischer was not a patient of mine, nor are there any psychological reports available from his brief consultations with psychiatrists, Dr. Harold Kline and Dr. Ariel Mengarini, during his youth/adolescence (discussed in Chapter Three).

Over the last two years as I have worked on the psychological autopsy section (Chapter Seven) of this book, I consulted on ethical issues with experienced leaders in the field of psychology, medicine, and law. These ongoing consultations facilitated self-monitoring of the ethical sensitivity and professional appropriateness of my research efforts. First, the psychologists thanked in the book "Acknowledgments" section were all asked to read my initial psychological autopsy (Ponterotto, 2011) and review my ethical cautions in offering a profile of an individual who was not my patient. I continued to consult with some of these colleagues throughout my research and writing process. Second, I had a phone conference consultation with Drs. Stephen Behnke and Lindsay Childress-Beatty of the American Psychological Association's Ethics Office, who helped me frame the methods, intent, and limitations of my psychological profiling of Bobby Fischer. Third, Fordham University's Institutional Review Board (IRB) reviewed and approved my methods and procedures for accessing and drawing on sensitive archival document analysis related to Bobby Fischer's family genealogy, including FBI files and psychiatric records.

From a medical ethics perspective, I received guidance from Dr. Marcus Zachary, D.O., former Chief of Medicine of Saint Francis hospital in San Francisco. Dr. Zachary emphasized, as did my psychologist colleagues, the need to appropriately bracket my psychological assessment, carefully document the sources of my information, and highlight the tentativeness and limitations of any diagnostic assessment. Finally, I met on multiple occasions with Joel Silverman, Esq., General Counsel of an international trading company, who read an earlier and much briefer version of this work and reviewed the ethical and legal appropriateness of my psychological assessment. These ethics consultations were helpful in guiding my work; however, I am fully responsible for the contents of this book.

RESEARCH METHODS

Probably more has been written about Bobby Fischer than any other chess player in history, including the renowned Paul Morphy and Jose Raoul Capablanca of centuries past, and Anatoly Karpov and Garry Kasparov of recent years. Though there are some biographical accounts of Bobby Fischer that are carefully researched and meticulously prepared (e.g., Brady, 1973, 2011; Edmonds & Eidinow, 2004; Kasparov, 2003) there is much more written about Bobby's life that is poorly researched and verified. In this book, I was careful to document all sources, and to triangulate both data collection methods and data information sources.

In terms of qualitative research methods to build the psychobiography, I relied on semi-structured and unstructured interviews, written document analysis, and review of audio- and videotapes made by or about Bobby Fischer. In terms of data information sources on Bobby, I relied on recollections of family members and acquaintances, close former friends, and various chess masters or chess insiders (e.g., tournament directors and sponsors and chess authors). Furthermore, I studied various biographies of Bobby Fischer and reviewed thousands of pages of documents on or about Bobby and his family as reflected in articles, book chapters, and an extensive FBI report on Bobby's mother, Regina Fischer. My research began in January, 2008, and ended with my review of the galley proofs for this book.

With a brief overview on the nature of psychobiography now provided, and with ethical considerations and research methods in hand, let us proceed to Chapter Two for the story of Bobby Fischer.

Chapter Two

DRAMATIC RISE AND MYSTERIOUS FALL OF BOBBY FISCHER

When he was at the board playing, it was like God was playing. The purity of his thought, the search for truth, the ability to go to the core of the problem. Bobby never looked for an easy move that would blow away his opponent. He looked for the truth in chess.
(Shelby Lyman as shared with Nicholas and Benson, 2003, p. 8)

Fischer demolished the Soviet machine but could build nothing in its place. He was an ideal challenger–but a disastrous champion.
(Garry Kasparov in *Wall Street Journal*, as cited in Evans, 2008)

BOBBY'S RISE TO THE WORLD TITLE

Robert James (Bobby) Fischer passed away of kidney failure at the age of 64 on January 17, 2008 in his adopted home of Reykjavik, Iceland, where, 36 years earlier, he had captivated the world with his stunning defeat of Boris Spassky, the reigning World Chess Champion from Russia. Bobby's 1972 victory in Reykjavik ignited in Americans a nationalistic pride perhaps not seen since Apollo 11 landed successfully on the moon in 1969, and not to be seen again until the underdog U.S. men's hockey team captured the gold medal in the 1980 Winter Olympics in Lake Placid, New York.

Bobby's genius at the game of chess, and his ascendency to the World Championship title in 1972, is well chronicled in various books (e.g., Brady, 1973; 2011) and documentary films (e.g., *Anything to Win:*

The Mad Genius of Bobby Fischer, 2004; *Bobby Fischer Against the World,* 2011). Appendix A of this book (see page 161) outlines a few milestones and major achievements in Bobby's chess career. Among the highlights likely already familiar to most chess fans worldwide is that Bobby started playing chess around the age of six, got really good around the age of eleven, was the U.S. Junior Champion at thirteen, and by fourteen years of age was the U.S. Chess Champion. Impressively, he won the U.S. Chess Champion eight times between 1958 and 1967 (see Brady, 1973). At the age of fifteen, after placing fifth in the Interzonal Tournament in Portoroz (formerly of Yugoslavia, and now part of Croatia), Bobby was awarded the title of International Grandmaster, the youngest person until that time, to be so honored.

In his final march toward the world chess title Fischer came in first in the Interzonal Tournament in 1970 in Palma de Majorca, Spain. Then Bobby had to play three 10-game candidate's matches against the world's top players to decide Spassky's 1972 challenger. First he dispatched the Russian Grandmaster Mark Taimanov by the score of 6–0. The Danish Grandmaster, Bent Larsen was next, and Fischer steamrolled him as well, again winning 6 games, while recording no losses or draws (6–0). The last hurdle before a world title match was the Armenian Grandmaster (representing the Soviet Union) and former World Champion, Tigran Petrosian. Fischer dominated this match, winning by a wide margin, $6\frac{1}{2}$–$2\frac{1}{2}$ (see Brady, 1973). Bobby Fischer had now earned the right to challenge Boris Spassky for the World Chess Championship.

Finally, in the summer of 1972 and in the midst of the Cold War period, Bobby at age 29, convincingly defeated ($12\frac{1}{2}$–$8\frac{1}{2}$) Boris Spassky in Reykjavik, Iceland to become the United States' first official World Champion.[1] Almost single-handedly Bobby Fischer broke what had been three decades of Soviet domination of the World Chess title. By September, 1972, Bobby Fischer was an international celebrity and superstar. Bobby now had the world at his feet–worldwide adoration, potentially millions of dollars in product endorsements, as much companionship (romantic or plutonic) as he desired–how would he now manage his genius, success, and fame?

Unfortunately, Bobby's life and story since his momentous 1972 triumph was sad if not tragic. While at the peak of his chess genius, Bobby lapsed into deeper and deeper states of anger, isolation, and paranoia that lasted until his death. After his riveting play in the 1972 championship match, the chess world was excited to follow his professional development and await his next display of "genius" at the board. Fans were soon sorely disappointed as Bobby withdrew from competitive chess and forfeited his world title in 1975 to Russian Grandmaster Anatoly Karpov. There would be no more stunning, innovative play by North America's first official world champion. And there would be no more brilliant Fischer games for chess players of all skill levels to replay across the chess clubs, coffee shops, schools, and living rooms of the world.

Bobby Fischer's ingenious play and unique personality had elevated the popularity of chess in the mid 1970s to an all-time high. Many high schools throughout the United States established chess clubs and strong chess players were finding employment teaching and tutoring chess. Membership in the United States Chess Federation (USCF) reached its all time high (up until that point in its history) of 60,000 members in 1972.[2] With Bobby's departure from active chess competition, America's new passion for the game subsided and leveled off. Bobby Fischer was, to many Americans, the face of chess, and in the 1970s there was no American superstar to assume the mantle.[3]

Bobby Fischer engenders strong emotive reactions in people. Some focus on his open hatred of Jews and his anti-American sentiments and wonder why he is still a topic of discussion. His anti-Semitism was simply unacceptable and his celebrating the September 11, 2001 terrorist attacks on the United States infuriated millions of people worldwide. At the other end of the spectrum there are those who, while not condoning his behavior and attitudes towards fellow humans, feel that Bobby should be honored for his chess accomplishments, and that his anti-Semitism and anti-Americanism should not detract from his place in chess history.

I witnessed firsthand the wide range of emotional reactions to Bobby Fischer. Last year, when I published my first article on Bobby Fischer (Ponterotto, 2011) in *Miller-McCune Magazine,* the responses and reactions from readers were strong and varied. There was one particular reaction to the article that caught my attention: an original poem written by Dr. Alfredo Pasin in Italy. Initially written by Dr. Pasin in Italian, he also translated the poem into English. With his permission I present the poem on the next pages. Furthermore, to acknowledge and honor the multilingual talent (and memory) of Bobby Fischer, his mother Regina Fischer, and his niece Elisabeth Targ, I present the poem, first in the original Italian, then in the English translation.

Il Giocatore Bobby

Vi prego non relegate me
Bobby, il giocatore di scacchi,
il piu' grande che il mondo conobbe
al solo ruolo
di pazzo paranoico alienato
fui questa la verita
un genio un artista un scienziato
vincitore feroce ma cortese
perdente raro cupo ma dignitoso
privo di lusinghe ed inganni
un artista guerriero
che viveva ancora
secondo le leggi dei samurai
in quell gioco piu ti tutto cercai
belezza armonia e verita
lo innalzai a vette infinite
ma non trovai mai
quiete e ristoro
alle mie pene di uomo
forse non fu la pazzia
e portarmi via
ma il vento nero e gelido
dell'Islanda
e delle sua malinconia

Dr. Alfredo Pasin, M.D.

Bobby the Chess Player

I beseech you, do not confine me,
Bobby, the chess player,
the greatest one the world could ever know
to the only role
of alienated crazy paranoid.
This was indeed the truth:
I was a genius, an artist and a scientist;
a winner ruthless but chivalrous
a rare loser, somber but still stout;
a warrior artist
free from flattery and cheats,
a warrior still living
according to the laws of Samurai.
In that game, what I have sought at most
'twas Beauty, Harmony and Truth:
I raised it to almost boundless heights
but I never encountered
quiet and replenishment.
Maybe it was not Madness
to bring me away
from my human sufferings;
'twas rather the dark and icy wind
of Iceland
and its melancholy.

Dr. Alfredo Pasin, M.D.

Dr. Pasin believes Bobby is the greatest chess player "the world could ever know" ("il piu' grande che il mondo conobbe"). How did Bobby Fischer get so good at the game of chess? How does Bobby's chess genius, talent, and accomplishments compare to other world champions? For my readers who may be a bit unfamiliar with chess history and its legacy of great champions, I end this chapter with first, a brief historical review of the origins of chess; second, I explore how Bobby Fischer got so damned good and, third, I evaluate Bobby's place and ranking among the world's chess champions.

BRIEF NOTE ON THE ORIGINS
OF CHESS AND ITS CHAMPIONS

The game of chess has been around for millennia. Perhaps the earliest predecessor to the game of chess was *senet,* played in the Stone Age as far back as 2000 BCE (Dean & Brady, 2010; Keene, 1990). Famed archeologist Howard Carter, who in 1922 unearthed the tomb of Tutankhamen, found three perfectly preserved games of senet. Senet includes 20 pieces played on a board with 30 squares. Individual Senet pieces look very similar to later-day chess pieces (see photos in Dean & Brady, 2010).

Some game historians believe that the immediate predecessor of chess was the Indian game of *chaturanga* (roughly 500 CE) which was a war game involving four players each working eight pieces. Each player controlled a maharaja (the modern day chess king), an elephant (a bishop), a horse (the knight), a chariot (a rook) and four foot soldiers (pawns). The game included rolling dice, and thus some aspect of luck was involved. Over time the four-person, eight-piece per-person game was collapsed into a two-person, sixteen-piece per-person game, without dice, and therefore without the factor of luck—it became a purely skill-based intellectual game of war. In the two-person collapsed version of the game, now called *chatrang,* the second king became a *vizier* (modern day queen). Thus, chess, as it is played today, likely originated in India, more specifically in the Indus Valley near the northwest border of India. Archaeologists have found chess pieces in the Indus valley dating back to the sixth century CE.

From India, the game of chess spread to Persia, then the Arab world in the seventh century, and then on to the Mediterranean countries in the early eighth century (Dean & Brady, 2010). It was in Europe where we have the Golden Age of chess and the first chess champions.

In the sixteenth century, as communication within Europe improved, and as it became safer to travel in Europe, international chess competition began. In 1560, Ruy Lopez, a priest from Extremadura, Spain visited Rome on church business. While in Rome he apparently played and defeated the most prominent Italian chess masters of the time (Keene, 1990). One of the first recognized international matches was between Spain and Italy in 1571 under the court of Philip II in

Madrid. In this two-country competition two Spanish and two Italian masters competed, and the Italian, Giovanni Leonardo emerged victorious. Leonardo was hailed as the first "champion of the Mediterranean countries" and the match signaled the start of the pre-world champion era (Kazic, 1974, p. 203).

Toward the late eighteenth and early nineteenth centuries, the dominant international rivalry was between France and England. The strongest chess players in this period were the Frenchmen: Philidor, Labourdonnais, and Saint-Amant; and Englishmen: Stamma (a Syrian emigree), McDonnell, and Staunton. In individual one-on-one matches Philidor, who defeated Stamma, Labourdonnais, who defeated McDonnell, and Staunton, who bested Saint-Amant, could all in their time be considered "champions of Western Europe."

Perhaps the first multination international tournament took place in 1851 in London in which 16 eminent masters from Western and Central Europe (France, England, Germany, and Hungary) took part. The winner of this tournament was the German player Adolph Anderssen, and he could be considered the "champion of Western and Central Europe." However, Anderssen was not "world" champion as the 1851 London tournament did not include competitors from the United States or Russia.

Seven years later, however, in 1858, when 21-year-old United States champion Paul Morphy traveled to Europe and played against the European champion, Adolph Anderssen in Paris, the first unofficial world champion was decided: Paul Morphy. Morphy defeated Anderssen by the score of 7–2 (with six wins, two draws, and one loss). After the Paris match in 1858, Paul Morphy was acknowledged by chess masters in Europe and the United States as the world champion. Unfortunately, Paul Morphy, like Bobby Fischer a century later, abandoned competitive chess after the championship match and fell into increasing states of mental illness. The story of Paul Morphy and its parallels to the story of Bobby Fischer is the subject of Chapter Eight.

GENIUS BLOSSOMS:
HOW DID BOBBY FISCHER GET SO GOOD?

Without question, Bobby Fischer was one of the greatest chess players who ever lived. How did he get so good? Was his chess genius innate, that is, genetically predisposed (the "nature" explanation in psychology)? Or perhaps, Bobby got great due to diligent study and practice at the game within the context of his early childhood and adolescent environment (the "nurture" explanation)? A third explanation would be an interactive combination of innate ability and environmental conditions coalescing to produce one of the world's greatest chess geniuses. As my reader likely already surmises, it is this third explanation that carries the most weight: Bobby Fischer got great due to natural innate abilities (that correlate with chess skill) anchoring diligent practice and study over many years and thousands of hours.

To understand how Bobby Fischer got so good at chess, it would be helpful to first briefly review some research on the development of expertise in general, and specific to chess mastery. On the "nature" explanation for chess mastery, chess prodigies likely have great natural talent which consists of an innate (genetically-predisposed) mixture of creativity, extreme competitiveness, visuospatial ability, and substantive IQ (Howard, 2005). Furthermore, there is a connection between childhood precocity for chess and eventual eminence at the game (Howard, 2008).

On the "nurture" side of the argument (that is, influences post-birth in the living environment), statistical models that weigh the influence of various predictors (of chess mastery), indicate that the most powerful statistical influence on elite chess skill or expertise is deliberate practice, defined often (but not always) as serious, purposeful chess study alone, in groups, and in serious chess play (Campitelli & Gobet, 2008; Charness, Tuffiash, Krampe, Reingold, & Vasyukova, 2005; de Bruin, Smits, Rikers, & Schmidt, 2008). A general consensus is that it takes about 10,000 hours of deliberate study often accrued in about 10 years to reach elite performance status, regardless of the activity (chess, violin, math, computer programming, music composition and so on) (see Gladwell, 2008 for a highly readable summary of the elite performers or the "outliers"). It appears it takes roughly 10,000 hours of focused effort for the human brain to absorb and integrate the necessary knowledge to become "world class" at some activity (Gladwell, 2008). The brain's focused concentration on the task in question for so many hours and years can lead to neurobiological changes in brain recognition and processing of information relevant to the specific task. More specifically, in recent neurobiological research using the latest rapid eye movement and functional magnetic resonance imaging (fMRI) techniques, it was found that experience and knowledge (likely gained through deliberate practice) in chess experts underlie rapid object recognition and possibly leads to different cognitive processes engaging additional brain areas not activated in nonexpert players (Bilalic, Kiesel, Pohl, Erb, & Grodd, 2011).

In addition to the primacy of deliberate practice in achieving task mastery, other variables appear to relate to elite chess skill. Studying adult tournament chess players of varying strength, Grabner, Stern, and Neubauer (2007) found general intelligence, and particularly numerical intelligence, also contributing to chess expertise. Interestingly, however, working with young chess players, Bilalic, McLeod, and Gobet (2007a) found that among children across broad skill levels, intelligence was a predictor of chess skill, but among a smaller subset of the best child players, intelligence and skill were not statistically related. It appears the relationship between IQ and chess ability is still uncertain and is probably mediated by a host of other variables such as age, type of intelligence being measured, level of skill, among other variables (Gobet & Charness, 2006).

As with intelligence and chess skill, the research on personality variables and chess expertise is limited and inconclusive. Intuitively, personality traits such as self-discipline, motivation, competitiveness, ambition and drive, and perseverance would relate to elite mastery of any specialized skill. Studying children, Bilalic, McLeod, and Gobet (2007b) found that boys who scored lower on the personality trait of "agreeableness" were more likely to take up the game of chess. Working with adult elite chess players, Vollstadt-Klein, Grimm, Kirsch, and Bilalic (2010) found that elite male players were more "introverted" than the normative national male population. In both of these studies, findings for female players were different, and thus gender appears to be a mediating variable between personality and chess interest and skill level.

With regard to Bobby Fischer, we can see the interaction of "nature" and "nurture" influences. Bobby's mother, Regina Fischer, and probably father, Dr. Paul Felix Nemenyi, were both intelligent, creative, scientifically skilled, and multilingual (promoting the ability to see and interpret events in various ways, with different perspectives and meanings; think of analyzing a chess position). Some of the innate abilities underlying such skills were likely passed along to Bobby.

With regard to deliberate practice, Bobby is a "poster person" for dedication and commitment to a singular skill and task: playing chess. As a child and adolescent, Bobby taught himself enough Russian, Serbo-Croatian, and other languages (see Brady, 2011) so that he could expand his library of chess literature and past games. Bobby played and studied chess hours a day starting around the age of seven when he got really interested in chess (he learned the moves at age 6); it is likely he had accrued 10,000 hours in less than 10 years, and in fact, by the age of 14 he was U.S. Chess Champion, and by the age of 15, a Grandmaster, the youngest person up until that time to receive such international acclaim in chess (see Brady, 2011).

For sure, personality characteristics and the home environment influenced Bobby's solitary life and his comfort around the chessboard. As will be discussed at length in subsequent chapters, Bobby was socially awkward, disliked school, had few close friends, and was often alone for long stretches of time during the day. Chess was his companion, his refuge, a place where he felt safe and protected from the frenetic life that characterized his home. Bobby was also good at chess, and his skill was a source of self-esteem, self-efficacy, and acknowledgement from people of all ages; these emotional rewards led Bobby further to the intense study of chess. Bobby's sense of "personal" identity became his "chess" identity. His innate ability, early life and family circumstances, and intense study and practice coalesced to form the foundation for chess genius. Was he the greatest chess player of all time?

BOBBY FISCHER'S PLACE AMONG THE WORLD CHAMPIONS OF CHESS

Bobby Fischer was the eleventh World Chess Champion and the first "official" champion from the United States of America. How does Bobby Fischer compare to other World Champions who came before and after him? Well, this is an age-old sports question and challenge of comparing talent across generations: Who was greater, Babe Ruth or Hank Aaron (baseball)? Jerry West or Michael Jordan (basketball)? Rocky Marciano or Muhammad Ali (boxing)? Pele or Lionel Messi (soccer)? Naturally there is some subjectivity and favoritism in claiming the world's best at anything. A young chess player today is more likely to consider a Kasparov, Karpov, or Fischer as history's greatest, rather than a Steinitz, Lasker, or Capablanca.

Though there is the challenge of comparing chess "greatness" across generations, statisticians have developed sophisticated rating systems that can provide some comparative estimates of chess strength across time. Perhaps the most accepted mathematical rating system was developed by Arpad Elo (1986), a professor of physics. The ELO system, adapted by FIDE in 1970, incorporates a statistical model that provides a game-to-game score for competitive chess players. Scores are adjusted after each official game with a rated player based on the ratings of opponents and total wins and losses. ELO ratings calculated on all the World Chess Champions up until 2003 (see Bohm & Jongkind, 2003) ranked Bobby Fischer (ELO = 2825) second after Garry Kasparov (ELO = 2850). ELO ratings as of July, 2011 (Wikipedia.org), ranked Fischer fifth among World Champions (ELO = 2785), behind Kasparov (ELO = 2851), Anand (ELO = 2817), Topalov (ELO = 2813), and Kramnik (ELO = 2811).

There is some criticism of rating inflation over time in the ELO rating system. To adjust for this concerns, Jeff Sonas developed a statistical model (see Chessmetrics.com) that attempts to control for rating inflation and also incorporates frequency of play. In Table 2.1 to follow, I list in chronological order all the "official" world champions in chess history and provide the average peak Chessmetric ratings over a ten-year, five-year, and single-year period.

As evident in Table 2.1, over a ten-year period, which is probably a more accurate measure of reliable chess skill and performance, the top five players, in order, were Kasparov, Lasker, Karpov, Capablanca, and Fischer. Over a five-year peak period there is a slight shift in rankings: Kasparov, Lasker, Capablanca, Botvinnik, and Fischer. However, looking at the final column of Table 2.1, the single year peak ratings, Bobby Fischer is ranked first (for his performance in 1972) followed by Kasparov, Botvinnik, Capablanca, and Lasker.

Most chess grandmasters who have played in the last half-century will agree that Bobby Fischer was one of the greatest players in the history of the game. For example, American Grandmaster Yasser Seirawan (2010) ranked Bobby Fischer as the third greatest chess player of all time (behind Kasparov and Karpov). Current World Champion,

Table 2.1
OFFICIAL WORLD CHESS CHAMPIONS (MEN) AND
THEIR CHESSMETRICS AVERAGE PEAK RATINGS

Undisputed World Champions (1886–1993)

		Average Peak Ratings		
Champion	*Championship Years*	*10 Years*	*5 Years*	*1 Year*
Wilhelm Steinitz	1886–1894	2763	2789	2802
Dr. Emanuel Lasker	1894–1921	2847	2854	2863
Jose Raoul Capablanca	1921–1927	2813	2843	2866
Dr. Alexander Alekhine	1927–1935	2804	2827	2851
	and 1937–1946			
Dr. Max Euwe	1935–1937	2731	2741	2759
Dr. Mikhail M. Botvinnik	1948–1957	2810	2843	2871
	and 1958–1960			
Vasily Smyslov	1957–1958	2776	2788	2794
Dr. Mikkail Tal	1960–1961	2763	2773	2793
Tigran Petrosian	1963–1969	2766	2782	2791
Boris Spassky	1969–1972	2759	2761	2771
Robert J. Fischer	1972–1975	2810	2841	2881
Anatoly Karpov	1975–1985	2821	2829	2842
Garry Kasparov	1985–1993	2863	2875	2879

FIDE World Champions (1993–2006)

Anatoly Karpov	1993–1999	2821	2829	2842
Alexander Khalifman	1999–2000	2700	2710	2721
Viswanathan Anand	2000–2002	2805	2818	2828
Ruslan Ponomariov	2002–2004	N/A*	2719	2753
Rustam Kasimdzhanov	2004–2005	N/A	N/A	2773
Vesselin Topalov	2005–2006	2738	2744	2773

Classical World Champions (broke from FIDE) (1993–2006)

Garry Kasparov	1993–2000	2863	2875	2879
Vladimir Kramnik	2000–2006	2798	2812	2822

Undisputed World Champions (FIDE and Classical United) (2006-Present)

Vladimir Kramnik	2006–2007	2798	2812	2822
Viswanathan Anand	2007–present	2805	2818	2828

*Data was unavailable on the Chessmetrics website.

Viswanathan Anand (2008) ranked Fischer second in chess history behind Garry Kasparov. Where Bobby Fischer stands in the ranking of chess greats is ultimately a subjective and personal opinion, but one that is clear: Bobby captured the attention and imagination of the world more than any player in the past century. Yet Bobby remains a mystery, an enigma, and in this book my goal is to explore this mystery and provide one window into the psychological life of an American legend. We begin with a look into his early childhood.

Chapter Three

IN THE BEGINNING:
THE EARLY LIFE OF BOBBY FISCHER

Bobby Fischer, I first met him in 1952, when he was only nine years old. Bobby was a blond, fair-complexioned, good-looking American boy, who was always dressed in a T-shirt and corduroy pants. When we were introduced, I noticed that he never looked up. I thought that he had, perhaps, dropped something and was still looking for it. But later, when he joined the Manhattan Chess Club, I noticed that he still could not make eye contact.

(Arnold Denker cited in Denker and Parr, 2009, p. 102)

BOBBY'S BIRTH AND FAMILY TREE

To understand Bobby's life, career success, and psychological history necessitates knowledge of the context and historical period in which he was brought into this world. This context included an immigrant, single mother–Regina Wender Fischer–raising Bobby and his older sister Joan in a near constant state of poverty during the height of the cold war period where Regina became a subject of FBI surveillance for suspected communist ties. Ongoing FBI surveillance (discussed in Chapter Four) hindered Regina's ability to find steady employment which, in part, led her to move the family from city to city in an ongoing search for work (see Brady, 2011).

For any child to be born into such a family and life context would be difficult and challenging; for Bobby, this was especially the case given his (genetically-predisposed) personality and temperament. As Bobby was an underdog to the mighty Soviet chess machine in the

1960s, so too was he, unfortunately, an underdog in his chances for a stable, balanced, and happy life.

Robert James (Bobby) Fischer was born at 2:39 P.M. on March 9, 1943 at Michael Reese Hospital in Chicago, Illinois (Brady, 1973). Figure 3.1 on the next page presents a partial family tree inclusive of five generations of the Fischer family. The family tree begins with Bobby's maternal great grandparents, moves to his grandparents (Jacob and Natalie Wender), and lists his mother's (Regina Wender Fischer) significant love relationships (Hans Gerhardt Fischer, Paul F. Nemenyi, and Cyril Pustan), as well as his own romantic partners in his adulthood (Zita Rajcsanyi, Miyoko Watai, Marilyn Young, and Petra Dautov).

Bobby's mother, Regina Wender, was of Polish-Jewish heritage born in Switzerland to Jacob and Natalie Wender on March 31, 1913. Bobby's biological father was most likely Paul Felix Nemenyi (also Jewish), a Hungarian physicist who met Regina in 1942 while working as an Assistant Professor of Mathematics in Colorado. However, Hans-Gerhardt Fischer, a German-born biophysicist whom Regina married in Moscow on November 4, 1933, was listed as Bobby's father on his birth certificate (Edmonds & Eidinow, 2004), and Hans-Gerhardt was assumed by the chess world to be Bobby's father until questions were raised in 2002. (I talk more about the debate over the identity of Bobby's biological father in Chapter Five.)

Bobby was the second of two children; he had an older sister Joan, five years his senior, born to Regina and Hans-Gerhardt Fischer in 1937 in Moscow where the couple was living at the time. As almost any chess fan in the United States knows, it was Joan who introduced Bobby to the game (Brady, 1973). The identity of Joan's biological father as Hans-Gerhardt Fischer is not in doubt. By all accounts, Hans-Gerhardt Fischer was totally absent in the lives of the Fischer children (Brady, 1973).[1]

BOBBY'S EARLY LIFE:
SEEDS OF PSYCHOLOGICAL CHALLENGE

Soon after Bobby's birth in 1943 Regina moved to Pullman, Washington (where Paul Nemenyi was living at the time), and then on to Moscow, Idaho, where in 1945 she legally divorced Hans Gerhardt

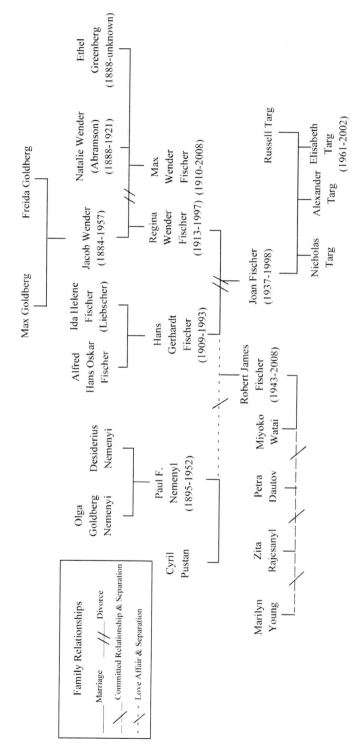

Figure 3.1. Robert (Bobby) James Fischer Family Genogram.

Fischer. Regina found odd jobs in these cities to support her family–stenographer, typist, and shipyard welder (Brady, 1973, 2011). From Idaho the Fischer family settled in Los Angeles where Regina worked as an elementary school teacher. The family then settled in the tiny town of Mobile in the Arizona desert about 35 miles southwest of Phoenix, where Regina continued work as a teacher. Though life in the Arizona desert was harsh (e.g., water was scarce), Joan Fischer remembered these years positively, reflecting to biographer Frank Brady, "It was the first place we were really happy" (Brady, 1973, p. 1).

From Mobile, Arizona, the Fischer family moved to New York City in 1948 where Regina Fischer, already a qualified Registered Nurse, pursued a Master's Degree in Nursing Education from New York University. The family first settled in Manhattan on East 13th street. It was on 13th street that Bobby's chess story begins. In March of 1949, the month of his sixth birthday, his sister Joan bought him an inexpensive chess set in the building's candy store, and together they learned the moves (Brady, 2011). Bobby had always liked games and puzzles (e.g., Parcheesi and Japanese Interlocking Rings), and initially his interest in chess was unremarkable, as he reflected years later to biographer Frank Brady: "At first it was just a game like any other, only a little more complicated" (Brady, 1973, p. 5). The family moved again in 1950 to Brooklyn, first finding an apartment on Union Street, one block south of Eastern Parkway, and then finally settling into a nearby four-room apartment (Apartment Q) in a four-story yellow brick building atop a barber shop and candy store located at 560 Lincoln Place, on the corner of Franklin Street (Brady, 1973; Ginzburg, 1962).

Bobby's early childhood was often disrupted by family moves from city to city. Long-time Fischer biographer Frank Brady (2011) documented that the Fischer family moved residences (across many different cities) 10 times during the first six years of young Bobby's life. Additionally, because of Regina's need to work, Bobby spent a lot of time alone. Brady (2011) noted that:

> Bobby was often alone. When he came home from school, it was usually to an empty apartment. His mother was at work during the days and sometimes in the evenings, and his sister was generally busy in school until later in the afternoon. Though Regina was concerned about her son, the simple truth was that Bobby was a latchkey child

who craved but was not given the maternal presence that might have helped him develop a sense of security. . . . And it didn't help that there was no father present. (p. 15)

The recollections of New York Chess Master and childhood friend of Bobby Fischer's, Allen Kaufman, supports Brady's (2011) memories. More specifically Kaufman shared the following memory with investigative journalists Nicholas and Benson (2003): "Joan was there, but mostly Bobby was just on his own and Regina was working, working all the time. She would work 24 hours at a time, and so Bobby was left rattling around, mostly on his own" (p. 4).

It appears Bobby never adjusted well to the New York City School system. As an elementary school student at Public School #3 (P.S. 3) on Christopher Street in Manhattan, Bobby was expelled when he kicked the school principal, Mr. Sallen (Targ, 2008). Bobby's brother-in-law, Russell Targ, who had also attended P.S. 3, reported to me that this incident took place when Bobby was around 6 years old. Bobby's older sister Joan, who was also a student at the school, withdrew after Bobby was expelled (Targ, personal communication, July 20, 2010). P.S. 3 was not the only school where Bobby had trouble adjusting and fitting in. According to Brady (2011), by the time Bobby reached fourth grade, he had been in and out of six different schools.

In contrast to his disinterest in public school, Bobby soon developed an intense interest in chess. In fact, to say Bobby soon became obsessed with chess would be an understatement. Since his early days in Mobile, Arizona, Bobby had been independent-minded and taciturn (Brady, 1973). Chess would further isolate him from typical childhood social activities and Regina soon became quite concerned with what she termed Bobby's "chess mania" (Brady, 1973, p. 8). More specifically,

she was worried that his interest in chess was becoming obsessive. She believed he was so engrossed in the game that he was never quite in touch with the reality around him, so addicted to chess that he would not—could not—control it, and that eventually, because of the exclusion of everything else, this accidental interest might ruin his life. (Brady, 2011, p. 28)

Regina's concern over Bobby's sole focus on chess led her to consult formally with two psychiatrists. First, she took Bobby to see Dr.

Harold Kline at the Children's Psychiatric Division of the Brooklyn Jewish Hospital. (Dr. Kline's obituary [*New York Times,* February 15, 1991], noted that he was both a pediatrician and psychiatrist specializing in child and adolescent care.) According to Fischer biographer Brady (2011), Dr. Kline told Regina that she need not worry, as many children of Bobby's age get intrigued and seemingly obsessed with particular games, toys, or sports. Kline went on to suggest that in time Bobby's obsession with chess would subside and he would take up other interests. Regina, however, was not satisfied with Dr. Kline's assessment. She knew her son better than anyone and she knew what other children Bobby's age were interested in. Regina sensed rightly that Bobby's obsession with chess was not just a passing developmental phase. So, Regina sought out a second professional opinion, this one from Dr. Ariel Mengarini, a government-employed neuropsychiatrist who also happened to be a chess master (Brady, 1973, 2011). However, and perhaps to Regina's dismay, Mengarini's assessment was similar to Dr. Kline's. Mengarini shared his memory of the event with Brady: "I told her I could think of a lot worse things than chess that a person could devote himself to and that she should let him find his own way" (Brady, 1973, p. 8).

Regina's sense of her son was prescient, and unfortunately her consultation with two different psychiatrists did not lead to psychological treatment for Bobby. The exact circumstances of the psychiatric consultations are not known, as obviously, the records of the sessions, if any exist, are confidential (I am not clear if the FBI ever interviewed Drs. Kline and Mengarini). One thing is clear: According to both Bobby's biographer, Brady (Personal Communication, June 25, 2010) and his brother-in-law Russell Targ (Personal Communication, July 20, 2010), Bobby never engaged in long-term counseling or psychotherapy. It may be, as suggested in Brady's (1973, 2011) biographies, that Drs. Kline and Mengarini normalized Bobby's behavior and did not recommend ongoing treatment. It is also possible that both psychiatrists offered to continue to meet with Bobby and/or Regina, but for some reason—cost, the fuss Bobby would make about going (and thus being taken away from his chess set), or some other circumstance—treatment was not initiated.

My educated guess as a practicing psychologist is that both Drs. Kline and Mengarini likely offered to continue to meet with Bobby and/or Regina given Regina's obvious upset and concern for Bobby, but that financial or transportation concerns, scheduling conflicts due to Regina's hectic work schedule, or simply Bobby's likely strong reluctance to continue, may have prevented further assessment and treatment.

Regina continued to be concerned for Bobby's well-being–his psychological health, his inattention to school, his lack of friends–and therefore continued to think about and problem-solve ways to get Bobby more support and help outside the arena of chess. One idea she had was to have Bobby meet informally (that is, not in a clinician-client relationship) with Dr. Reuben Fine, a psychoanalyst and world class chess grandmaster.[2] Regina reasoned correctly that Bobby would surely like to meet and play chess with Dr. Fine, a chess legend. Soon after Bobby won the 1956 U.S. Junior chess championship at the age of 13, Regina approached Dr. Fine to discuss Bobby's chess obsession and requested that he spend some time with Bobby in a mentoring role. In his book *Bobby Fischer's Conquest of the World's Chess Championship,* Fine (2008, pp. 24–25) described a telling anecdote about his subsequent meetings with Bobby:

> He came to see me about half a dozen times. Each time we played chess for an hour or two. In order to maintain a relationship with him I had to win, which I did. . . . My family remembers how furious he was after each encounter, muttering that I was 'lucky.' Hopeful that I might help him to develop in other directions, I started a conversation at one point about what he was doing in school. As soon as school was mentioned, he became furious, screamed 'You have tricked me' and promptly walked out. For years afterward, whenever I met him in clubs or tournaments he gave me angry looks, as though I had done him some immeasurable harm by trying to get a little closer to him.

This exaggerated and perhaps paranoid reaction to Dr. Fine's overture reflects a pattern of Bobby's interpersonal style that would be a hallmark of his adolescent and adult behavior. Over the years, Bobby made many close friends in the chess world, and more often than not, at some point during the friendships, he cut them out of his life believing they had betrayed his trust in some way. Unfortunately, Bobby also at times cut out of his life his own family members–his mother Regina, his sister Joan, and his brother-in-law, Russell Targ–for stretches of time. Bobby Fischer would become distrustful of almost all the significant associations in his life.

In Chapters Six and Seven, I delve more deeply into the "psychology" of Bobby Fischer. However, a preliminary step in understanding Bobby's inner emotional world is to understand more fully his parents, and the nature of Bobby's relationship to them. Bobby's markedly ambivalent relationship with his mother Regina (Chapter Four) and his lack of an ongoing relationship with his (probable) father, Paul Nemenyi, is at the heart of his inner psychic struggles. Therefore, to understand Bobby Fischer, we first must know his parents.

Chapter Four

MOTHER LOVE: UNDERSTANDING REGINA FISCHER'S RELATIONSHIP WITH SON BOBBY

Whenever Regina came to the Manhattan Chess Club, Bobby always bolted for the door in embarrassment. Mind you, Bobby was never rowdy. Far from it. He behaved well, but when something happened with which he couldn't cope, he headed for the hills like a spooked horse.
(Arnold Denker cited in Denker and Parr, 2009, p. 103)

The most dominant and powerful piece on the chess board is the queen. In many ways the chess queen is an icon of female power. The "queen," translated into Italian or Latin is "regina." Interestingly, the most powerful force and influence in Bobby Fischer's life was his mother, Regina Fischer. Without question, Regina had a significant impact on Bobby's career development and personality. With regard to his chess career, Bobby's ascendency to chess preeminence may not have occurred without Regina's support and advocacy. Regina's son-in-law, Russell Targ, remarked to me confidently that "Bobby would not have been world champion without Regina" (Russell Targ, personal communication, August 10, 2010). Though this is only the opinion of Mr. Targ, it is noteworthy, given that he likely knew the Fischer family better than anyone currently alive. With regard to Regina's influence on Bobby's emotional and personality development, the story is more layered and complex, and understanding more deeply this mother-son relationship is the primary goal of this chapter.

More specifically, this chapter opens with a symbolic comparison of Regina Fischer to the influential and powerful queen on the chessboard. Next, a brief profile of Regina Fischer as a mother, peace activist, and health professional is provided, and the stress she endured as a subject of decades of FBI surveillance is highlighted. This section integrates summaries of the FBI's most recently released (March, 2011) and updated 994-page file on Dr. Regina (Wender) Fischer (Pustan). Third, this chapter highlights the limitations of the FBI files and promotes a more balanced and contextualized profile of Regina Fischer. To this end, in the fourth and final section of the chapter, an in-depth psychological profile of Regina Fischer is presented, one that incorporates the historical, cultural, political, and economic context that helps explain and perhaps normalize much of Mrs. Fischer's attitudes and behavior.

REGINA FISCHER: QUEEN MOTHER

Recently, I was reading Marilyn Yalom's (2004) book entitled *Birth of the Chess Queen: A History*. Marilyn Yalom, an established author, is a senior scholar at the Institute for Women and Gender at Stanford University. Coincidentally, Marilyn is married to Irvin Yalom, the world renowned existential psychiatrist and author. It was Irvin who introduced Marilyn to the game of chess. In reading Yalom's interesting book, a number of her descriptions or characterizations of the chess queen reminded me of the force, power, and family dedication of Regina Fischer. Consider the following quotes from Yalom's work:

> The chess queen is an awesome warrior who can move in any direction—forward, backward, to the right, to the left, and diagonally—one space at a time or across the entire board. In a microcosm where all movement is strictly regulated, she defies the narrow constraints that bind the rest of her army. (pp. xvii–xviii)

> Initially, she sits at the side of the king, as befits a royal spouse. During the game, she charges forth to protect her lord and destroy their enemies. If necessary she may give her life in combat, for ultimately it is the king's survival that counts. This is the paradox of chess: he is the crucial figure, even if she is more potent. (p. xviii)

Above all, the chess queen is dangerous, awe-inspiring, unpredictable. She often makes the difference between life and death. Each time she moves, her opponent shudders: 'Beware, here comes the queen.' (p. 238)

Though the "warrior" depiction may not apply to Regina Fischer, other characteristics of Yalom's descriptions of the chess queen do apply, either literally or symbolically. Regina was a "mover," literally, fleeing both Germany (from the Nazis) and the Soviet Union (from Stalin's purges), moving throughout the United States to find employment, returning back to Europe to finish medical school, participating in a year-long nuclear disarmament peace walk from San Francisco to Moscow, working as a pediatric physician in England, Germany, Portugal, Honduras, and Nicaragua, and returning back to family in Palo Alto, California. She also defied the strict conventions of mothering in the 1940s in terms of her educational and career pursuits, constant travel and protesting of various causes, her forceful personality, and her outspoken advocacy on behalf of U.S. chess generally, and son Bobby, specifically.

Symbolically, like a queen for her king, Regina risked her health to support her son when she went on a six-day hunger strike to draw attention to the financial needs of U.S chess players (Brady, 2011). And though her acquaintances did not likely "shudder" when she stepped into a room, they always knew when she was present and that she would speak her mind and take action to support her son. Stalwarts of the American chess community who knew her well, Jack Collins, Dr. Frank Brady, Carmine Nigro, Dr. Anthony Saidy, Arnold Denker, among others, understood well the strength of her character and convictions (see Brady, 1973, 2011; Denker & Parr, 2009; Saidy, 2004, 2011).

Regina Fischer as Peace Activist, Mother, and Subject of FBI Surveillance

Regina Fischer was highly talented, widely educated, and multilingual. In fact, she had full fluency or at least a working knowledge of six languages (English, French, German, Portuguese, Spanish, and Russian) (FBI Report #65–1236). Regina's intellectual curiosity, educational drive, social justice commitment, and passion to serve others was extraordinary. After raising Joan and Bobby as a single parent, Regina returned to East Germany to continue her medical studies. She received her M.D. in 1968 at the age of 55 (see Fine, 2008), and even went on to earn a second doctorate, this one a Ph.D. in Hematology (Frank Brady, personal communication, June 28, 2010).

A life priority for Regina Fischer was social justice and peace activism. As her daughter Joan Fischer Targ once remarked: "my mother is a professional protester" (Brady, 2011, p. 87). In the early 1960s, Regina protested against nuclear weapons across cities, countries, and continents, and a decade later she moved on to protest the Vietnam War. In 1973 Regina was arrested in Paris, France for protesting the Vietnam war (FBI Report # 100–3218). Then in 1977 she was arrested in London while campaigning against the deportation of two Americans detained as a threat to national security (Edmonds & Eidinow, 2004). Throughout her life, Regina Fischer maintained the courage and forcefulness to stand up and speak out on causes she deeply believed in—social justice, peace, and supporting her children.

Raising Joan and Bobby as a single parent in the 1940s and 1950s was understandably challenging. Though she worked whenever she could and had some financial support from Bobby's (likely) biological father, Dr. Paul Nemenyi, and from her own father Jacob Wender, Regina still struggled to provide for her family. Layered on top of her responsibilities as a single mother with limited financial means, in the post-Depression, Cold War, Anti-Semitic context of the United States in the mid-1900s, Regina Fischer had to deal with almost relentless FBI surveillance. One can only imagine the collective stress weighing on the shoulders of Mrs. Fischer.

FBI Investigation Begins

FBI surveillance of Regina Fischer began in October of 1942, five months before giving birth to son Bobby. Given Regina's pregnancy and precarious financial situation, along with the absence of family members who could care for five-year-old daughter Joan for extended periods of time, Regina endeavored to place Joan in temporary foster care in St. Louis while she moved to Chicago to prepare for Bobby's birth. On October 1, 1942, Regina dropped Joan off at her foster placement sponsored by the Sommers Children's Bureau, a Jewish Welfare Agency. The foster mother, while looking through a box of

Joan's belongings left by Regina, became alarmed by some of the contents of the box. Among the items left with Joan's clothing was a letter indicating that Regina Fischer "had been confined in the New York Hospital of incipient tuberculosis, being released there from in May, 1941." The foster mother also found documents with various chemical formulas on them, as well as a camera, a camera stand, two rubber sheets, and a rubber glove (FBI Report # SL 65–1236, p. 1–2). Fearing that Joan may have been vulnerable to catching tuberculosis from her mother Regina, and feeling concerned by the odd material in Joan's clothing box, the foster mother demanded that the Sommers Children's Bureau remove Joan from her home. The foster mother then contacted the FBI regarding her suspicions regarding the items in the box. Thus, on October 3, 1942, the FBI began what would extend to three decades of investigation of Regina Fischer.

It is understandable given the later context of the Cold War period why Regina Fischer would raise suspicion in the FBI. First, Regina and her husband Gerhardt Fischer lived in Russia for an extended period of time (1933–1939) and had high-level scientific training. Second, since returning to the United States in 1939 Regina Fischer had "a substantial record of association with Communists and Communist sympathizers [and] she was recruited in the Communist Political Association in Portland, Oregon, in 1945" (FBI Report # NY 100– 102290). (Regina was expelled from the Communist Political Association sometime prior to April, 1953 for not being "a faithful party member" [FBI Report # 100–102290].) Third, the FBI uncovered strong evidence that Regina's husband, Gerhardt Fischer, was active in the communist party in Chile where he settled in 1940, and they believed that he may have been a spy for Russia (FBI Report #NY 100-102290).[1]

During their three decades of surveillance of Regina Fischer, FBI agents in various cities and states (and a few countries) interviewed many individuals in an attempt to ascertain if in fact Regina Fischer was a Soviet spy. The tenor of the FBI reports generally portrayed Regina in a negative light in terms of her personality characteristics, her parenting skills and relationship with son Bobby, her collegial relationships, and her mental health. For example, one FBI informant in conversations with Regina Fischer "gained the impression that she has little or no control over her son, who apparently rebels and resents any parental supervision and is both temperamental and uncooperative."

The source then "described Regina Fischer as a very talkative individual who apparently cannot control her son and, therefore, also lives in terror of him but at the same time seems to 'gloat' over his publicity" (FBI Report # NY 100–102290).

Another FBI source, who appears to have lived or worked at the Fischers' 560 Lincoln Place, Brooklyn address, described Regina as "a very strange and peculiar individual . . . that Regina Fischer apparently has a 'suit complex,' and has on many occasions during the period she has resided at 560 Lincoln Place, sued the landlord for imagined grievances." The source goes on to describe "Regina Fischer as an antagonistic, argumentative, untruthful individual and stated that the Fischers are disliked by all the tenants in the apartment house. She further stated Regina Fischer apparently has no close friends" (FBI Report # NY 100–102290).

Apparently, according to FBI informants, Regina's sense of independence and autonomy presented challenges to some university officials, as Regina hoped to design her own curriculum and be exempt from general curricular standards. More specifically, during 1954–1955 when Regina attended the School of Nursing at Teachers College, Columbia University, she had some conflicts with academic advisors. An FBI summary report indicated that Regina was placed on a "special list," which meant she

> could not register in the Teachers College without special permission because of a departmental recommendation based upon her continued refusal to accept guidance and her attempts to change the above school curriculum to suit her personal whims. (FBI Report # NY 100–102290, p. 4)

In June of 1943, three months after the birth of her son Bobby, Regina received a mandated mental health evaluation after being arrested for disturbing the peace. The incident stemmed from a disturbance caused by Regina when she and baby Bobby lived at a Chicago charity for indigent single women and their babies–the Sarah Hackett Memorial Home. Regina had placed Joan in the care of her father, Jacob Wender, during her delivery (Brady, 2011). However, she soon had Joan rejoin her and infant Bobby at the Sarah Hackett Memorial Home, which was against policy as the residence was only for mothers and their newborn infants. When Regina demanded that

Joan be allowed to stay, the authorities were called in (FBI Report # CG 100–27015, pp. 8–9).

The mandated mental health evaluation was conducted at the Municipal Psychiatric Institute in Chicago on June 22, 1943, and the attending mental health professional diagnosed Regina Fischer as a "stilted (paranoid) personality, querulent [sic] but not psychotic." The report noted that "It is difficult to see how she can unravel the complexities of her personal life. It is obvious that she will continue to refuse any agency or counsel. If her small children should suffer because of her obstinacy, juvenile court intervention should be initiated'" (FBI Report # 65–45667–52, # NY 100–102290, and # CG 100–27015). It is important to note that this psychiatric diagnosis uncovered by FBI agents in Chicago has never been confirmed by any mental health professional outside the Municipal Psychiatric Institute.[2]

Ambivalence in the Mother-Son Relationship–Regina Fischer Moves Out

Until the age of 17, Regina Fischer was omnipresent in Bobby's life. However, as Bobby grew into adolescence and young adulthood he clashed with his mother more frequently and directly. Eventually, Bobby and Regina could no longer live together and in October, 1960 when Bobby was 17, Regina moved out of their 560 Lincoln Place, Brooklyn apartment to live with a female friend at 1804 Longfellow Avenue in the Bronx (FBI Report # NY 100–102290, p. 1).[3] In an interview Bobby gave to journalist Ralph Ginzburg in August, 1961 when Bobby was 18 years old, he discussed the circumstances of his break from his mother.

Fischer: "After that [becoming designated an International Grandmaster in 1958] I quit school."

Ginzburg: "How did your mother feel about that?"

Fischer: "She and I just don't see eye-to-eye together. She's a square. She keeps telling me that I'm too interested in chess, that I should get friends outside of chess, you can't make a living from chess, that I should finish high school and all that nonsense. She keeps in my hair and I don't like people in my hair, you know, so I had to get rid of her."

Ginzburg: "You mean that she moved out of the Brooklyn apartment you lived in?"

Fischer: "Yeh, she moved in with her girlfriend in the Bronx and I kept the apartment. But right now she's away on this trip with those people [the pacifists] for about eight months. I don't have anything to do with her" (Ginzburg, 1962, p. 52).

In addition to his views on his mother, Bobby is also quoted in the Ginzburg interview sharing anti-female and homophobic sentiments. It should be noted that Bobby was very upset and angered by Ginzburg's (1962) article and denied to biographer Dr. Frank Brady that he had made some of the quoted statements. Dr. Brady, in fact, approached Ginzburg to request the audiotapes to hear for himself what Bobby actually said in the interview. Ginzburg responded to Brady that the audiotapes had been destroyed (Brady, personal communication, July 13, 2010). In his updated biography of Fischer, Brady (2011) was critical of Ginzburg's reporting and interpretation of the infamous interview. Talking about the veracity of Ginzburg's quotes, Brady stated:

> One can never know the full truth, of course, but even if Ginzburg merely reported verbatim what Bobby had said, it was a cruel piece of journalism, a penned mugging, in that it made a vulnerable teenager appear uneducated, homophobic, and misogynistic, none of which was a true portrait. Previous to this, Bobby had already been wary of journalists. The Ginzburg article, though, sent him into permanent fury and created a distrust of reporters that lasted the rest of his life (p. 139)

Despite Bobby's specific comments in the Ginzburg interview, it was clear he had an ambivalent, and an on and off again relationship with his mother in terms of regular contact. In his often viewed "Park Bench Interview" (see Bobby Fischer Against the World, 2011), Bobby, in responding to the interviewer's question about his mother, stated that "I haven't seen her in a few years." Though some published reports had stated that Bobby and his mother were estranged for up to ten years, there is now ample evidence that Bobby and Regina maintained some level of contact throughout Regina's life (see Brady, 2011; Evans, 2003; Weber, 2008).

Just a few examples of Bobby's ongoing contact with his mother include the following. In 1968 after an aborted tournament in Lugano, Switzerland (Bobby quit the event when one of his tournament demands was not met) he flew to Germany to visit his mother who had moved there to finish her medical degree (Brady, 1973). Journalists Quinn and Hamilton (2008) noted that Regina Fischer turned "up in Iceland [at the 1972 World Chess Championship] disguised in a blonde wig to witness his [Bobby's] finest hour, in defiance of his orders to stay away" (p. 1). Brady (2011) also mentioned that Regina showed up in Iceland to support Bobby and stayed for one day and evening, sleeping in Bobby's suite at the Loftleidir hotel. In Brady's (2011) new biography of Bobby Fischer, there is a photo of Regina (in wig) and Bobby sitting across from one another at a chess table in Bobby's room and smiling at the photographer.

It is not certain how Bobby felt about his mother's visit during the 1972 match. In his new book of photos on Bobby Fischer, Harry Benson, his long-time photographer (from photo shoots in Buenos Aires, November, 1972; Grossinger's resort, Liberty, New York, May, 1972; and Reykjavik, Iceland, June-September, 1972) and friend, recalled he and Bobby passing Regina Fischer in the lobby of Bobby's Reykjavik hotel: "I once saw Bobby merely nod to his mother in passing as he walked through the lobby of the Loftleidir hotel. Perhaps they visited together later when I wasn't there, but I never saw it" (Benson, 2011, pp. 70–71).

It is now clear that during the 1992 rematch with Spassky, Bobby was in contact with his mother. More specifically, one of Solotaroff's (1992) interviewees (Jezdimr Vasiljevic, the 1992 match organizer) shared that Bobby was in regular phone contact with both Regina and his sister Joan.

Regina also spent time with her son in the late 1980s when Bobby was living in the Los Angeles area. At that time, Regina's granddaughter, Dr. Elisabeth Targ was completing her psychiatric residency at UCLA and living in Santa Monica. Elisabeth and her then boyfriend, Dr. Robert Lipton, would on occasion help care for both Regina and Bobby. Dr. Lipton, who is now an Associate Professor of Psychology in the Department of Emergency Medicine at the University of Michigan, Ann Arbor, recently shared with me his first memory of seeing Bobby Fischer:

> I saw him walking hand-in-hand with Regina down the block towards Elisabeth's apartment in Santa Monica. Bobby is big and awkwardly put together, Regina was relatively tiny and bent over; it was

a very touching moment. (Robert Lipton, personal communication, March 5, 2011)

This scene depicts the tenderness between Bobby and his mother Regina and provides a sharp contrast to the perception in the FBI reports that Regina and Bobby were always in a state of tension.

And finally, to the very end of Bobby's life as he lay critically ill in a Reykjavik hospital, he was thinking of his mother Regina, as reflected upon by his brother-in-law Russell Targ:

> Late in the evening of Thursday, January 17, 2008, I received a phone call from Gardar Sverrisson, Bobby's neighbor and one of his closest friends of the last few years. He told me Bobby had died in the hospital that evening. I knew Bobby had been very ill. The previous week, our family had sent him photos of his mother Regina at his request. (Targ, 2008, p. 239)

Limitations of FBI Perspective and a More Balanced Profile of Regina Fischer

Cold War Context of FBI Investigation

Much of the writing on Regina Fischer, including some of my own (Ponterotto, 2011), has presented a negative, diagnostic slant. This was due to a reliance on the FBI reports as a major source of information on the life and personality of Regina Fischer. It is important to keep in mind the anti-communist fervor in the United States in the mid-twentieth century. President Harry Truman's Executive Order 9835 (also known as the loyalty order or the loyalty test) in 1947, and President Dwight D. Eisenhower's Executive Order 10450 (also called the suitability test) in 1953, fed a nationwide communist paranoia. During this period, Senator Joseph McCarthy was vigorously leading investigations into "anti-American" activities. The fear of communist infiltration filtered down from the federal government, the state department, and the FBI to the average citizen.

This was also a time when certain immigrant ethnic groups were more likely to be associated with communism. The conviction (in 1951) and execution (in 1953) of American Jews, Julius and Ethel Rosenberg, for conspiracy to commit espionage was front-and-center in the public's mind. Obviously, the Fischer family was Jewish and as noted by chess master and Bobby Fischer long-time friend Shelby Lyman: "This was a time when Jews and communists were equated" (Lyman, 2011).

Thus in learning of the life and activities of Regina Fischer, it is important to note a natural bias likely reflected in the FBI investigation. To be sure, the 994-page FBI dossier on Regina Fischer is a valuable source of information given the meticulous, almost obsessive recording of events and interviews by FBI field agents, and given their unfettered access to almost everything about Regina including birth and immigration records, academic and employment records, housing records, and of course, interview access to family, friends, associates, and colleagues. My sense was that few people turned down an interview request by the FBI during the height of their investigation of Regina Fischer.

To balance the FBI reporting on Regina Fischer I took care to interview people who knew her well. These individuals included Fischer biographer Dr. Frank Brady, long-time Fischer friend Dr. Anthony Saidy, and especially family intimates, Russell Targ (Bobby's brother-in-law) and Dr. Robert Lipton (the former boyfriend of Regina's granddaughter, Dr. Elisabeth Fischer Targ). Through these interviews I have come to see more of Regina's psychological strengths, her force of character and conviction, her resiliency and her devotion to her children (and causes she believed in). A more balanced, layered, and accurate profile of Regina Fischer has emerged.

A More Balanced Perspective on Regina Fischer

It is clear that Regina deeply loved her son Bobby (and daughter Joan) and did her best to provide for and support Bobby throughout his life. Regina had her own challenging psychological history, was often struggling financially, and was harassed and dogged by FBI surveillance. This FBI surveillance, which lasted for decades, was a form of harassment for Regina Fischer. FBI agents would interview Regina's colleagues and associates and this intrusion hindered Regina's efforts to find steady employment (Russell Targ, personal communication, August 10, 2010). Furthermore, FBI agents even interviewed friends and extended family members of Regina's. For example, they interviewed Regina's stepmother, Ethel (Greenberg) Wender in 1958 (FBI Report # SL 65–45667–78), and her son-in-law Russell Targ in 1959

(FBI Report # NY 100–102290, pp. 42–45). Given the stigma associated with being an FBI subject of inquiry during the Cold War period, one can surmise that the FBI intrusion in Regina's life further isolated her from some sources of social support.

Despite financial hardships and the ongoing stress of decades of FBI surveillance, Regina raised two "successful" children and received both M.D. and Ph.D. degrees. Bobby, despite his psychological challenges and at times tortured life, was certainly, for a short period at least, successful in his career–World Chess Champion. And Regina's daughter Joan went on to a teaching career, a happy family, raising with her husband Russell Targ three well-adjusted and highly successful children, two of whom became physicians–Elisabeth Targ, a psychiatrist and published scholar (Sicher, Targ, Moore, & Smith, 1998), and Alexander Targ, an anesthesiologist–and one an attorney, Nicholas Targ, who is also a published scholar (e.g., Hill, & Wolfson, & Targ, 2004). Russell Targ provided descriptive and career profiles of his three children in his autobiography (Targ, 2008).

Regina understandably had ambivalent feelings toward her son Bobby's chess career. On the one hand, early on she encouraged Bobby to broaden his interest and friendship base beyond chess. However, as Bobby's genius for chess became more apparent in his early adolescence, Regina did all she could to support his chess passion and pursuits. Knowing of Bobby's social skills deficits, his awkward interpersonal style, and his ignorance (as a child and adolescent) of topics outside of chess, Regina may have believed chess was the route to Bobby's career and financial sustenance. Regina knew well the hardship of financial struggle and she did not want Bobby or Joan to experience such hardships in their lives.

Regina was often involved in protests and demonstrations salient to supporting Bobby's chess career and promoting the status of chess in the United States. A good example was in the 1960s when she picketed the White House because the U. S. State Department refused the national chess team's request to play in the 1960 Chess Olympiad in East Germany (FBI Report # 65–45667). Though Bobby was at times embarrassed by his mother's forceful advocacy behavior, it is clear she loved him deeply and was a staunch supporter of Bobby's chess career (Brady, 1973, 2004, 2011).

Regina Fischer died of cancer in 1997 at the age of 84 in Palo Alto, California. Sadly, Bobby's older sister Joan (who was married to Russell Targ) died of a cerebral hemorrhage a year later in 1998 at the age of 60 in Portola Valley, California (Targ, 2008). Unfortunately, due to his fugitive status, Bobby could not return to the United States to attend the funerals. As I will discuss in latter chapters, these two losses, coming so close in time, may have had a significant impact on Bobby's developing psychological state.

Understanding the Psychology of Regina Fischer

Fully understanding Bobby Fischer necessitates a deep understanding of his relationship with his mother. Regina Fischer's approach to parenting, to social relations outside her family, and to her work ethic are naturally influenced by her own family and cultural history.[4] Her way of being in the world (and her world view, or the lens with which she sees, interprets, and behaves in her world) is impacted by the experiences of the Holocaust generation and those that preceded it. Furthermore, Bobby Fischer, and Joan Fischer Targ and her offspring, are also impacted by the life experiences and world view of Regina Fischer and her ancestors.

Therefore, in understanding the complex psychological life of Bobby Fischer it would be helpful to explore the life and possible world view elements of his mother Regina Fischer, who figured so prominently in his life. In this section I hypothesize sociocultural-religious aspects of the life of Regina Fischer that may help to put her world view and behaviors, as well as those of her son Bobby, into deeper and more accurate perspective. A good place to start is on understanding important aspects of Regina Fischer's early life, including her relationship with her own parents/stepparent.

Regina Fischer's Early Childhood and Adolescence

Regina Fischer's last memory of her mother, Natalie (Abramson) Wender, was when she was five years old: she pictures her mother lying in bed, apparently ill and nonresponsive. According to Regina's early life memories, which were recorded and saved by her family (N. Targ, 2000), Regina told family members that her mother had died in 1918 during the great flu pandemic. The FBI files (in multiple entries) report that Natalie Wender died in 1923 (e.g., FBI Report #NY 100– 102290, p. 2). In actuality, Natalie Wender died on October 26, 1921 while a long-term patient at New Jersey State Hospital at Morris Plains (Greystone Park), New Jersey. In 1921, New Jersey State Hospital was known as the "New Jersey State Lunatic Asylum at Morristown"; it took the "Greystone Park" name in 1924 (Wikipedia). I was able to view Natalie Wender's death certificate, signed by Dr. Laurence Collins, who attended Natalie from March 1, 1919 to her death on October 26, 1921.[5] The death notice states that Natalie had resided at this facility for 3 years, 4 months, and 26 days, which means she arrived in June, 1918. The death certificate lists Natalie's age at death at 37 years, and notes her husband as "Jacob Wender"; further it specifies the maiden name of "Abramson." We can be confident that this is the same Natalie Wender that was Regina Fischer's mother. Furthermore, the 1920 U.S. Federal Census also reports Natalie Wender living at the psychiatric hospital. While at the hospital (according to the 1920 U.S. Federal Census taker, Mary R. Keegan) she was able to work in the laundry room, which indicates a certain level of functioning.[6]

This information, however, is all that is public and available to researchers, and we do not know her diagnosis upon admittance to Greystone, her course of treatment, or when psychiatric symptoms first appeared prior to hospitalization.[7] It is also unclear if Regina Fischer knew the truth about her mother's illness and final years and kept it from her daughter Joan's family, or whether, perhaps, her father, Jacob Wender, never told Regina (or her brother Max) the truth of her mother's mental illness and death.

On October 24, 1919, Regina and her older brother Max were admitted to the Brooklyn (Kings County) Hebrew Orphan Asylum (Case #M-19544; www.ancestry.com). No doubt, due to Natalie's illness and hospitalization, Jacob Wender could not care for his children. It is known from stories passed on from Regina to her grandson Nicholas Targ (2000), that the orphanage experience was difficult for Regina and Max. It is likely that some of the origins of Regina's social justice commitment stemmed from these difficult experiences.

Regina and Max would live at the orphanage some 18 months until they were discharged on April 7, 1921. At discharge, Regina and Max were accompanied to the train station with name tags attached to their coat buttons, and placed on a train to St. Louis, Missouri, where they were met by their father, Jacob Wender. Upon arriving home in St. Louis, Regina and Max were introduced to their future stepmother, Ethel Wender and her two children, Herman and Sylvia.

According to Regina Fischer's recollections of this time, initially she and her brother Max got along well in the blended family. However, over time, and due to financial strains between Jacob and Ethel, family tension rose considerably. Interestingly, in the FBI files which document two marriages (1923 and 1945) and two divorces (1934 and 1957) between Jacob and Ethel, financial strain and tension is noted in the divorce proceedings (FBI Report # SL: 65–1236, pp. 1–2).

Soon Regina and her brother Max were not getting along well with their stepmother, Ethel (Greenberg) Wender. Regina confided to Jewish Family Service staff that she left home as a teenager to live with friends. Furthermore, in an April 8th, 1958 FBI interview, Ethel (Greenberg) Wender reported that she had no contact with Regina or her brother Max Wender for 25 or 30 years and knew nothing of their activities. Ethel Wender went on to state that "she had never gotten along with her two stepchildren and that they moved away from home when they were still in high school" (FBI Report # SL 65–1236, p. 2).

Regina was a very bright child and teenager, and in fact she graduated Soldon High School in St. Louis, Missouri at the age of 15. She attended the University of Colorado from 1931 until 1932 when she withdrew and moved to Berlin, Germany where her brother Max was living at the time. Regina would eventually return to the University of Colorado in 1941 and received her Bachelor's degree on August 23rd, 1941 with a distributed [triple] major in Zoology, Chemistry, and German. Her Undergraduate Grade Point Average was 1.93 on a 2.0 scale and she ranked 19 and 1/2 out of 71 graduates. Regina also scored the highest grade on her New York State Nursing Exam, and received a Regent's Scholarship to continue her education and become a nurse educator (FBI Reports # NY 100–102290, p. 5, and # 65–45667096, pp. 1–2).

Regina Meets Gerhardt Fischer

Soon after she arrived in Berlin, Germany in 1932, Regina met her future husband–Hans Gerhardt Fischer. According to his birth certificate, Hans Gerhardt Joachim (Liebscher Fischer) was born on October

3, 1908.[8] His father, Alfred Hans Oskar Fischer, and mother, Ida Helene Fischer nee Liebscher, listed their religions as "Evangelisch," or Protestant in English. Therefore, it is clear that Hans Gerhardt was not Jewish as this was a question left unresolved in previous Fischer biographies. In 1933, Regina and Hans Gerhardt relocated to Moscow where Hans Gerhardt found employment at the Moscow Brain Institute and Regina began medical school at the First Moscow Medical Institute. Regina and Hans Gerhardt married in 1933, and in 1937 Regina gave birth to daughter Joan.

Eventually, as World War II approached, the Fischer family did not feel safe in Moscow where the Stalin purges were well underway, and Regina and Joan moved to Paris, France in 1938 to be joined by Hans Gerhardt in 1939. Soon, Paris too was threatened as the Nazi rise continued and Regina, who was a naturalized citizen of the United States returned to New York with daughter Joan. Hans Gerhardt, as a German citizen who had fought on the side of the Communists in the Spanish Civil War, was not allowed into the United States at that time—he found safe haven in Chile using a Spanish passport he had secured earlier (see Brady, 2011, and FBI Report # NY 100–102290, pp. 11–12).

It is not clear how much Regina was in love with her husband Hans Gerhardt when she left for the United States with Joan. One thing is clear: Hans Gerhardt did not support Regina and Joan financially. Hans Gerhardt's lack of support of his wife and daughter may have been due to his own financial struggles in Chile, or to a process of distancing himself emotionally from Regina. In Chile, Hans Gerhardt supported himself working in fluorescent lighting and in photography. As a highly educated scientist, this level of underemployment must have been difficult for Hans Gerhardt.

Regina as a Single Mother

By the early 1940s it appeared that Regina was either no longer in love with Hans Gerhardt or, for practical reasons, was separating from him emotionally. Evidence from extensive Jewish Family Services staff interviews with Regina in the early 1940s, and documented in the multiple FBI reports, indicated that she wanted to divorce Hans Gerhardt (which she eventually does in 1945 in Moscow, Idaho), and that she was, in fact, in love with Dr. Paul Nemenyi, a Hungarian Jewish refugee who was a doctoral-trained mechanical engineer and physicist (FBI Report # CG 100–27015, p. 9). The two had met in Denver, Colorado and started a relationship. (I talk much more about the men in Regina's life–Hans Gerhardt Fischer and Paul Felix Nemenyi–in Chapter Five).

From 1939 through 1950, we know that Regina and her two children Joan (born in 1937) and Bobby (born in 1943) were in constant motion. Bobby Fischer biographer, Dr. Frank Brady (2011), traced Regina through 10 cities by the time Bobby was ten years old. Why did Regina move so frequently? For one, Regina was constantly in search of gainful employment and she traveled wherever she had to in finding work. Second, FBI agents began surveillance of Regina in 1942, and their harassment (e.g., interviewing friends, associates, employers; landlords/building superintendants) hindered her ability to find steady work. Russell Targ, Regina's son-in-law, shared with me that Regina long-knew she was being followed and surveilled by FBI agents in multiple cities (Russell Targ, personal communication, August 10, 2010). In fact, on October 29, 1953, FBI agents approached Regina about consenting to an interview. She was uncooperative with the agents, stating that she had nothing to hide, but would only speak with them with her own legal counsel present (FBI Report # 100–102290, p. 69).

Third, some of Regina's moves may have been, in part, efforts to be close to Paul Nemenyi, her lover and Bobby's likely father. Nemenyi was also moving from city to city in his efforts to find steady employment. Regina was somewhat dependent on Nemenyi for financial assistance, and he provided some level of financial support to Regina for many years. For example, it is clear from FBI files that Paul Nemenyi paid for a rental apartment for the Fischer family in Pullman, Washington near where he was working in 1944 (FBI Report # CG 100–27015). Furthermore, Dr. Nemenyi arranged to have money sent to Regina (ostensibly to help support her and his son Bobby) regularly through Jewish Family Services in various cities (FBI Report # NY 100–102290, p. 26).

Psychologically speaking, moving from city to city to find safety, employment, and social connection was not new to Regina Fischer, as she needed to flee in a previous context of escaping Nazi or Stalin's persecution. In the 1930s, she had fled Berlin for Moscow, Moscow for

Paris, and Paris for the United States. In some ways Regina's peripatetic nature had been a successful coping and survival strategy.

Another personality and behavior characteristic of Regina that was perhaps part of her Holocaust history, was both a need to reach out for help from people she may not have necessarily known very well, accompanied by concerns over trusting the intentions of others. Specifically, Regina was often reaching out to others for help, particularly for financial assistance. During Bobby's youth and/or adolescence she had reached out to Jewish Family Service centers in at least four cities, to her father Jacob Wender, to her lover Paul Nemenyi, and to many in the chess community for various types of support, particularly as it concerned son Bobby. Among the renowned elders in the chess community that she reached out to for some kind of support included Carmine Nigro, John (Jack) and Ethel Collins, Dr. Frank Brady, Dr. Anthony Saidy, Arnold Denker, Dr. Reuben Fine, Dr. Ariel Mengarini, among others (see Brady, 1973, 2011; Denker & Parr, 2009). In approaching the chess community, Regina was advocating for her son Bobby who needed financial assistance and career support.

Regina also called on chess elders to help her "reach" Bobby in various ways for at times she did not feel Bobby would listen to her. An example here is when Regina called Dr. Anthony Saidy, a close friend of Bobby's and an International Chess Master, asking for his help in convincing Bobby to appear on a television game show *I've Got a Secret* to raise travel funds; Regina did not think Bobby would listen to her and thought Dr. Saidy could persuade him (Saidy, 2004, 2011).

Culturally speaking, Holocaust survivors and refugees had to at times rely on the grace of others for help in securing safe passage, getting hold of certain documents, gaining access to critical information (e.g., safe border crossings), finding hiding spots–it was literally a matter of survival. So too Regina had to rely on the help of others as a single working parent of two children during the post-Depression era and under the unrelenting stress of FBI surveillance.

However, relying on others at times was risky. Historically, many Jews in Europe were "turned in" to Nazi authorities, apparently betrayed by neighbors, colleagues, and even former friends as the latter attempted to gain favor with the Nazi authorities. Thus for some Holocaust survivors a marked ambivalence develops around the question of trust. The individual needs others for her own and her family's survival but is not sure who is really to be trusted.

Though in the United States, Regina was not escaping Nazi persecution, she still had, as part of her world view and weltanschauung, the ambivalence of both needing others but not fully trusting their intentions. And Regina had good reason to be weary and distrustful of some Americans. As discussed earlier in this chapter, shortly before giving birth to Bobby, Regina found herself the subject of virtual full-time FBI surveillance. She escaped the Nazis in Europe, and now in her own country, she is hunted (symbolically) again, this time by the FBI who suspected (wrongfully) that she and her husband Hans Gerhardt Fischer may have been Russian spies. Apparently, Regina could not trust the foster mother who was to care for Joan while Regina prepared for the birth of son Bobby in Chicago. It was the foster mother who reported Regina to the FBI believing she had found suspicious documents among Joan's belongings.

Furthermore, Regina, and eventually Bobby, were distrustful of the leadership of the American Chess Foundation, as they believed the foundation was backing Samuel Reshevsky, not Bobby, as the country's best hope to break the Russian hegemony over the World Chess Championship (Brady, personal communication, February 8, 2011). As will be discussed in Chapter Six, issues of trust and ambivalence were a hallmark of Bobby Fischer's personality development.

SUMMARY

Regina Fischer was a forceful, outspoken, ambitious, and driven woman who marched to her own drum, resisted conventional expectations, and confronted authority when she felt it unjust to herself, her family, or those with less political power in society. Regina Fischer was highly intelligent, highly educated, and multilingual, and she devoted much of her career to helping others as a nurse and physician. Clearly, she was fiercely committed to supporting the less fortunate through her social justice and peace activism. Some of Regina Fischer's personality traits are reflected in her son Bobby, who also marched to his own drum, rebelled against authority, whether it be FIDE or the U.S. government, and "did it alone," often being mistrustful of others. Bobby Fischer was also highly intelligent, multilingual, and highly educated in one career arena: Chess.

A number of Regina Fischer's traits are also reflected in her daughter Joan Fischer Targ and her three grandchildren. Joan became a nurse and teacher, and also fought relentlessly for causes she believed in, as exemplified in her six-year legal battle to create an organic vegetable garden on the Targs' Portola Valley, California property (see Targ, 2008). Regina's granddaughter, Dr. Elisabeth Targ was multilingual and devoted her career as a psychiatrist to helping others in direct service and through distance healing methods (see Sicher, Targ, Moore, & Smith, 1998). Regina's grandson Alexander is also a healer– a physician and pediatric anesthesiologist. Interestingly, like his grandmother Regina, Alexander (known as Sandy to family and close friends) is a "mover"–he has a mobile anesthesiologist practice anchored in his adapted SUV (Targ, 2008). And Nicholas Targ, a successful attorney, dedicates much of his professional skill to environmental and human rights issues, as reflected in his co-editing a special issue of *Human Rights* magazine on American Indian/Alaska Native Issues (Dean & Targ, 2006).

To honor the memory of Dr. Regina (Wender) Fischer (Pustan) I end this chapter with three quotes, not from the 994-page FBI File on Regina, but from three individuals who knew her well personally: Russell Targ, Dr. Anthony Saidy, and Dr. Robert Lipton. These reflections provide a more balanced profile of Regina's character and mental health than is reflected in the FBI files.

> Regina did not display any signs of mental illness during the forty years of my friendship and association with her. (Russell Targ, personal communication, August 7, 2010)

> Regina was a bulldozer of a woman and wasn't much interested in another's view point . . . I never saw her out of her equilibrium, angry, sad, or defensive. (Dr. Anthony Saidy, personal communication, March 28, 2011)

> Regina was quite a determined woman, very ideologically driven; she was by no means unkind, but she was also not super personable either; [this is not to be] taken to mean she was cold or personally unresponsive, she just had a different way of interacting, mostly through ideas and action. (Dr. Robert Lipton, personal communication, March 6, 2011)

Chapter Five

WHO IS MY FATHER? THE MYSTERY
OF BOBBY FISCHER'S PATERNITY

Everyone knows that Bobby Fischer had a very difficult childhood. No father, a harried mother, you name it. Many a night, Regina Fischer telephoned me in worry about where Bobby was. She did not understand until too late that chess was his savior because it helped him dissipate pent up aggression.

(Arnold Denker cited in Denker and Parr, 2009, p. 103)

From Bobby Fischer's birth in 1943 until roughly 2002, some 60 years, the chess world believed Hans Gerhardt Fischer to be Bobby's biological father. After all, Regina Fischer had told hospital officials that Hans Gerhardt was the father and thus his name was listed as the father on Bobby's birth certificate. In more recent years, however, mounting evidence has emerged that leads most Bobby Fischer researchers to conclude that Dr. Paul Felix Nemenyi was Bobby's actual biological father. It should be acknowledged at the outset, that it was the groundbreaking investigative reporting of former Philadelphia Inquirer reporters Peter Nicholas (now with the *Los Angeles Times*) and Clea Benson (now with *Bloomberg News*) that uncovered the FBI evidence of Bobby's father's true identity. Many journalists and biographers (including myself) have used Nicholas and Benson's research findings as a springboard for our own investigative work.

In this chapter, the evidence as to the paternity of Bobby Fischer is summarized. The chapter opens with a brief profile of Regina's first husband, Hans Gerhardt Fischer, and then moves to explore clusters of evidence supporting the conclusion that Dr. Nemenyi was in fact Bobby's father. As will be discussed at length in Chapters Six and Seven, Regina Fischer's secrecy about the identity of Bobby's father, as well as Bobby's lack of an ongoing consistent relationship with a father figure, would have significant implications on his psychological development.

WHO WAS HANS GERHARDT FISCHER?

Hans Gerhardt Joachim (Liebscher Fischer) was a German-born biophysicist who had first met Regina Wender (Fischer) in 1932 when she visited her brother Max in Berlin, Germany (FBI Report # NY 100–102290, p. 24). Fearing the Nazi rise in Germany, Hans Gerhardt moved to Moscow where he secured employment at the Moscow Brain Institute. Regina also moved to Moscow to attend medical school at the First Moscow Medical Institute, where she studied from 1933–1938. Regina and Hans Gerhardt dated in Moscow and married in 1933; Regina was 20 years old at the time. Four years later, in 1937, Hans Gerhardt and Regina had a baby daughter, Joan.

In 1938 as World War II approached and Stalin's purges were in full bloom (see www.bbc.co.uk/history_figures/stalin_joseph.shtml), Regina and baby Joan moved to Paris thinking it a safer haven; shortly thereafter they were joined by Hans Gerhardt. However, soon it was clear that Paris was not safe from the Nazi onslaught and Regina and baby Joan returned to the United States. As a German citizen who was suspected by the FBI of being a Soviet spy, Hans Gerhardt was not permitted entry into the United States to rejoin Regina and Joan; he eventually settled in Chile. FBI investigation indicated that Hans Gerhardt, using the name Gerardo in Chile, arrived in Los Andes, Chile from France on January 4th, 1940. By 1945 he was settled in Santiago, Chile, working as a photographer. He reportedly was a member of the Communist Party in Chile (FBI Report # NY 100– 102290, p. 11).

It is not clear how much contact Regina and Joan maintained with Hans Gerhardt after their arrival in New York in 1939. There appears to have been some early mail correspondence between Regina and Hans Gerhardt, but the extent of their communication is unclear. With their physical separation, Regina and Hans Gerhardt became estranged and Regina sued for and received a legal divorce from Hans Gerhardt in 1945 while she was living in Moscow, Idaho. There is no indication that Hans Gerhardt sent financial aid to Regina and Joan. Furthermore, biographers of Bobby Fischer appear confident that Hans Gerhardt was not at all involved in contacting or supporting Bobby after his birth in 1943 (Brady, 1973, 2011; Edmonds & Eidinow, 2004).

Hans Gerhardt's daughter Joan, however, did in time have some contact with her father. FBI inquiry identified travel dates and flight numbers of Joan's trip to Santiago, Chile in 1958, presumably to reunite with her father Hans Gerhardt (FBI Report # 65–45662–92, p. 1). Further evidence that Joan was in contact with her father came from her husband, Russell Targ. According to Targ, who would marry Joan Fischer in 1958, Joan went to visit Hans Gerhardt for a full year soon after they started dating. At some point in the year 1957, Russell had suggested in a letter to Joan that they get married. Apparently, Joan discussed Russell's marriage idea with her father Hans Gerhardt. Interestingly, Targ (2008) described in his autobiography Joan's parents' reactions to his idea of marriage:

> Joan and her physicist father Gerhardt Fischer discussed the idea for several weeks and decided that I looked like a good prospect. He had been a pioneer in the development of the EEG (brain waves) in Germany, before he and Regina left for the USSR in 1933, to keep a step ahead of the Nazis. (The same year Albert Einstein left.) Regina, on the other hand, was opposed to our marriage. She wanted to know why her beautiful and talented daughter chose a blind man to marry. (pp. 84–85)

Years later, when I interviewed Russell Targ (personal communication, July 20, 2010), I asked him about Regina's concern about his marriage proposal to Joan. Russell shared with me that Regina was concerned that his visual impairment (described in Targ, 2008) might impede his ability to be a good financial provider for her daughter Joan. As was discussed in earlier chapters, Regina struggled financially for most of her life, and thus it is understandable that she would be concerned for the financial welfare of both her talented and bright daughter and her bright but troubled son.

THE IDENTITY OF BOBBY'S BIOLOGICAL FATHER

While it is clear that Hans Gerhardt Fischer was Joan's biological father, the debate over the true identity of Bobby's Fischer biological father continues. However, most of the biographers and journalists, as well as the FBI, who have comprehensively studied the Fischer family history, believe that Paul Felix Nemenyi was Bobby's biological father.

Interestingly, in his updated biography of Fischer, Frank Brady (2011) does not commit to identifying Bobby's father, and instead proposes three paternity scenarios. First, he offers that Paul Nemenyi may indeed be the father. Second, he states that Regina may have traveled to Mexico in June of 1942 to meet up with Hans Gerhardt and the two had a sexual union that could have led to Regina's pregnancy with Bobby. Brady's third scenario is that perhaps Regina Fischer did not know who Bobby's father was, intimating that Regina may have had multiple lovers during the summer of 1942.

Of these three scenarios, it is my strong belief that the latter two scenarios put forth by Brady (2011) are highly unlikely. My rationale for believing Paul Nemenyi to be Bobby's biological father is outlined below. I venture that the probabilities of Brady's three scenarios are as follows: Paul Nemenyi as father, 90 percent, Hans Gerhardt Fischer as father, 5 percent, and unknown father, 5 percent.

EVIDENCE FOR PAUL FELIX NEMENYI BEING BOBBY FISCHER'S BIOLOGICAL FATHER

Paul Felix Nemenyi was a Jewish man born in Fiume (that time a part of Hungary) on June 5, 1895 (Truesdell, 1952), thus he would have been some 18 years older than Regina Fischer. Paul Nemenyi received his doctoral degree in Engineering at the Berlin Institute of Technology in 1922. He then lectured on various engineering subjects at technical schools in Berlin until he was stripped of his academic position for being Jewish as the Nazis rose to power (see also Nicholas & Benson, 2003).

Nemenyi fled to Copenhagen, Denmark, where he found work teaching engineering. From Denmark Dr. Nemenyi traveled to Great Britain, and on June 1st, 1939 he emigrated to the United States (FBI

Report # NY 100–102290, p. 62). According to the News and Notes archives of the *American Mathematical Monthly* (1944, 1947) as well as an article on "The Migration of Mathematicians" (Dresden, 1942), upon arriving in the United States, Dr. Nemenyi lectured at a number of colleges and universities in the United States, then worked in hydraulic research in Iowa, and eventually became an instructor at Colorado State College in 1941. In 1944 he was appointed instructor at the State College of Washington (in Pullman); in 1947 he was appointed physicist at the Naval Ordnance Laboratory in White Oak, Maryland, and at his death on March 1, 1952 he held the esteemed position of Head of the Theoretical Mechanics Section of the Naval Research Laboratory in Washington D.C. Dr. Nemenyi died at the age of 56, just four days shy of his 57th birthday (Truesdell, 1952). At the moment of his death, Dr. Nemenyi was at a dance in the International Student House in Washington DC. He suddenly collapsed and died of "coronary insufficiency" (FBI Report # WFO 100–27777, p. 3).

By various accounts, Dr. Nemenyi was a brilliant and visionary scholar in mechanics and physics. He was an international expert in five related fields: static elasticity, fluid dynamics, hydrology and hydraulics, organization of mechanics, and methods of research in investigating mechanics. Among his many discoveries was the proof of the following theorem, "Given any set of isothermal curves, there exists a five-parameter family of plane stress systems for which these curves are stress trajectories." This analytic proof was deemed brilliant by his scientific peers and was thus given the formal name "Nemenyi's theorem" (Truesdell, 1952, p. 215). One of his former students, who also became an eminent scientist, Dr. C. A. Truesdell, a colleague at the Naval Research Laboratory, prepared a detailed tribute to Dr. Nemenyi in an obituary published in *Science* (Truesdell, 1952).

The reason I present some detail on the intelligence and analytic prowess of Dr. Nemenyi, is because we see some of these same traits in Bobby Fischer, albeit the fluidity, connectedness, and the advanced visual inference ability is applied to another challenging intellectual field: chess.

Dr. Paul Nemenyi had a son Peter through an earlier marriage, and at the time of his father's death in 1952 Peter was a Ph.D. student in mathematics at Princeton University. Peter, who was roughly 15 years older than Bobby, would be his half-brother, that is, having the same father but a different mother. Like his father Paul, Peter went on to a promising scientific and publishing career. In addition to his scientific aptitude, Peter was also a human rights and social justice activist. In fact, in the 1960s he was beaten and arrested while helping Black Americans integrate local coffee shops (Nicholas & Benson, 2003). Peter Nemenyi had high levels of mathematical aptitude and scientific talent, and also had deep levels of empathy for oppressed persons. Peter Nemenyi committed suicide in 2002, a topic that will be discussed in Chapter Seven.

In the early 1940s while Dr. Paul Nemenyi was an instructor of mathematics at Colorado State College in Boulder, Colorado, he met Regina Fischer who was a student at the University of Denver (FBI Report # NY 100–102990, p. 26). The two began dating and it is highly probable that in the summer of 1942 Paul Nemenyi and Regina Fischer had a sexual union that would lead to the birth of one of the greatest analytic minds of the twentieth century–Robert James Fischer. In 1942, Dr. Nemenyi would have been around 47 years old, and Regina, 29 years old.

In recent years, with updated FBI files on Regina Fischer [that is, previously redacted text in the files was made available after Bobby's death in 2008], and with Fischer family intimates speaking more openly since the passing of both Regina and Bobby Fischer, a preponderance of evidence leads to the logical conclusion that Paul Nemenyi was Bobby Fischer's biological father. Below I review nine clusters of evidence that leads me to this conclusion.

First, evidence suggests that Hans Gerhardt and Regina, though not legally divorced until 1945, had no confirmed contact since 1939. During this seven-year period Hans Gerhardt was living in Chile and working as a photographer. Despite Brady's (2011) hypothesis that Regina may have flown to Mexico for a meeting (and a possible sexual assignation with Hans Gerhardt took place), I have found no records indicating that Regina traveled to Mexico in the summer of 1942. The FBI files on Regina tracked her travels, passport applications and numbers, and no where in the 994-page dossier is there any indication that Regina traveled to Mexico in 1942. There is however, documentation that Regina traveled to Mexico City with son Bobby from January 21 through February 11, 1959 (FBI Report # NY 100–102290, p. 1).

Second, there is ample evidence from FBI reports of interviews with Jewish Family Services workers and from friends of Regina Fischer, that Dr. Paul Nemenyi had ongoing contact with Regina the year before Bobby's birth in 1943 and soon thereafter when Regina moved the family to Pullman, Washington, where Paul Nemenyi was then living. Furthermore, evidence also indicated that Paul Nemenyi visited with Bobby on occasion until his death in 1952 (FBI Report # WFO 100–27777, p. 1).

Third, according to FBI documents, Regina told a Jewish Family service social worker that: "In1940, while at the University of Denver, she met Paul Nemenyi and in 1943, gave birth to a boy by Nemenyi" (FBI Document # NY 100–102290, p. 24). Paul Nemenyi had also confided to a social worker that he was Bobby's father, as evident in the notes of the FBI report:

> Nemenyi, at that time, advised that he first met the subject [Regina Fischer], while she was studying at the University of Denver. A friendly relationship ensued and subject subsequently became pregnant. Nemenyi stated they had agreed to put the child up for adoption, but subject later refused. (FBI Document # NY 100-102290, p. 26)

Fourth, there is documentation that Paul Nemenyi used the Jewish Family Service agency in various cities (e.g., Los Angeles, Washington, DC, and New York) to both deliver money to Regina and Bobby, and to express his concern for the welfare of Bobby. In one FBI report, a social service worker told the FBI agent that

> Nemenyi suffered a great deal when he was with the subject [Regina Fischer] and was emotionally upset to the point of weeping during the interview with her. She advised he was upset because the child, in his opinion, was not being brought up in desirable circumstances due to the instability of the mother. (FBI Report # NY 100-102290, p. 26)

Fifth, in letters written to and by Peter Nemenyi, the son of Paul Nemenyi (who donated the letters to the Wisconsin Historical Society), Paul is identified or implicated as Bobby's father. In one letter written by Peter (then a Princeton University student) the month after

Paul's death (Bobby would have been 9 years old), he wrote to Dr. Harold Kline (known to have been Bobby's psychiatrist in New York [though we do not know how often Dr. Kline met with Bobby]) "asking for advice on who should inform Bobby of Nemenyi's death; he assumed the doctor knew that Nemenyi was Bobby's father" (Edmonds & Eidinow, 2004, p. 321; see also Nicholas & Benson, 2002). The entire text of this letter, dated March 13, 1952, is presented below:

> Dear Dr. Kline:
> I am writing to you for some advice on a question concerning Bobby Fischer. Paul Nemenyi died recently (March 1st). I take it you know that Paul was Bobby Fischer's father. The question arises from a telegram that Bobby's mother, Mrs. Regina Fischer, sent me with the request to tell Bobby the news for her. I don't feel qualified to do it, because I hardly know Bobby at all, having only met him twice (and only briefly) and because I have no idea at all of what his inner life and orientation is like. The matter is further complicated by the false pretenses about Bobby's identity and the parents' differences of opinion over this question. I fear that I would be reinforcing the lie by taking the job of notifying Bobby about Paul's death from the mother. On the other hand I don't want to say no unconditionally, as I am not sufficiently familiar with the situation. I should therefore like to ask you either to advise me on this matter, or to tell the mother to notify Bobby, or to do it yourself, whichever you think is the right course. If you would do this for me, I should be very grateful. I have written to Regina Fischer, telling her that I don't feel qualified to break the news to Bobby and that I am writing to you for advice.
> Sincerely yours,
> Peter Nemenyi (son of Paul Nemenyi)" (Reprinted by permission of the Wisconsin Historical Society Archives, Peter Nemenyi Papers).

This letter is interesting on a number of levels. First it adds more evidence that, indeed, Paul Nemenyi was Bobby's biological father. Second, it also reveals the depths of empathy and thoughtfulness of Peter Nemenyi. Many others in his situation, might have simply dismissed Regina Fischer's request in her telegram, saying something like, "I hardly knew Bobby; he was your son; you tell him that his father is dead." Instead, Peter considers the request which is disconcerting to him; he takes the time to write this thoughtful letter to Dr. Kline, and he leaves some window in the letter that dependent on Dr. Kline's response, he might be willing to be further involved. The thoughtfulness evident in this letter by Peter, coupled with his history of civil rights activism, gives some indication of his caring, empathic character. This impression is reinforced by the memories of his good friend Sheila Michaels, who knew Peter from 1961 until his death in 2002. Her reflections highlighted Peter's humbleness, empathic nature, and lifelong commitment to equal rights for minority populations (Peter Nemenyi [1927–2002]: Memories, at www.crmvet.org/mem/nemenyi .htm).

Peter's caring nature reminds us of his father Paul's emotional turmoil (documented in FBI agent interviews with social workers at various Jewish family service offers) over concern for Bobby's welfare given his perceptions of Regina's instability and frenetic life. It seems that Paul Nemenyi and his son Peter were caring, thoughtful, and empathic individuals, in addition to being intellectually gifted and highly educated.

Sixth, approximately a month after Peter Nemenyi's letter was written, Regina Fischer wrote to Peter asking if his father had left any money for Bobby. Specifically she stated the following:

> Bobby . . . was sick 2 days with fever and sore throat and of course a doctor of medicine was out of the question. . . . I don't think Paul would have wanted to leave Bobby this way and would ask you most urgently to let me know if Paul left anything for Bobby. (Nicholas & Benson, 2002, p. A1)

Seventh, researchers Nicholas and Benson, in addition to being the first journalists to request Regina Fischer's FBI file under the Freedom of Information Act, also requested and received the FBI file on Regina's husband, Gerhardt Fischer (reported in Nicholas, 2009). In the file there was a letter dated May 22, 1959, written by FBI Director, J. Edgar Hoover and addressed to Allen W. Dulles, the Director of the CIA. The letter stated

> It is interesting to note that investigation has established that the father of Robert James Fischer is not [Gerhardt] Fischer as represented by Mrs. Fischer. Investigation has established that Robert James Fischer's father was one Paul Felix Nemenyi. (cited in Nicholas, 2009, p. 4)

Eight, when Paul Nemenyi died without a will, a probate court document submitted by Nemenyi's estate with the intent of asking Regina Fischer to give up any claim to Nemenyi's estate was filed in the District of Columbia. In that document (which Regina Fischer did sign), the following point was included:

> that one Robert Fischer, a minor, living with his mother Regina Fischer, at 560 Lincoln Place, New York City, was born to the decedent out of wedlock and that said Robert Fischer is not an heir and does not claim to be an heir of the above decedent and that said Regina Fischer is not the wife and does not claim to be the wife of the above named decedent. (FBI Report # WFO 100–27777, pp. 3–4)

Ninth, though perhaps less convincing than the above evidence, Paul Nemenyi had a striking physical resemblance to Bobby which became apparent in Bobby's adulthood. The first Bobby Fischer researchers to notice the marked physical similarities between Bobby and Dr. Paul Nemenyi were the journalists Clea Benson and Peter Nicholas in the year 2005. Clea Benson had discovered mail correspondence between Dr. Nemenyi and his colleague, the Hungarian-born engineer, Dr. Theodore von Karman that was archived at the California Institute of Technology. Benson contacted the Cal Tech archivist and received copies of correspondence between the two renowned scientists, and among the items sent was a photo of Paul Nemenyi. Upon seeing the photo, Benson and Nicholas (who work together on their Bobby Fischer research) noted that "the resemblance to Bobby was striking: the same deep-set burning eyes, the same facial structure, even the same unruly shock of hair" (cited in Nicholas, 2009, p. 4).

Furthermore, FBI reports described Nemenyi as having a large nose, large knobby fingers, and an awkward, slovenly walk and dress. Some of these physical descriptions have been applied to Bobby, though he was quite particular about his dress (preferring imported, handmade suits and shoes; see Ginzburg [1962]) from about 1960 through 1972, though not before or after. I invite my readers to assess for themselves the physical similarities between Paul Nemenyi and Bobby Fischer as reflected in the photos presented in Plates 5 and 6 (pages 79–80).

In one of my discussions with Russell Targ (personal communication, July 20, 2010), Bobby's brother-in-law, he believed that, in fact,

Paul Nemenyi was likely Bobby's biological father. He based this opinion on (1) the ongoing contact between Regina and Paul during Bobby's early years, and (2) the intellectual similarity between Paul and Bobby in terms of a gift for spatial visualization.

Finally, Peter Nemenyi shared with friend Sheila Michaels that his father Paul had indeed started a second family in the United States, and that Bobby Fischer was his father's son. According to Sheila, "Peter remembered [Bobby] with some fondness, although their philosophies could not have been more at odds." Apparently, Peter at times babysat for Bobby and their father, Paul Nemenyi, likely wanted Peter and Bobby to get to know each other (Sheila Michaels, www.crmvet.org/mem/nemenyi.htm).

In summary, though we cannot be 100 percent certain without genetic testing, there is a plethora of convincing evidence that Paul Felix Nemenyi was Bobby's biological father. It is for this reason that I estimate the probability of Paul Nemenyi being Bobby's biological father as high as 90 percent, whereas the probability that Hans Gerhardt Fischer (5%) or an unknown father (5%) is practically negligible.

DID BOBBY KNOW THE IDENTITY
OF HIS BIOLOGICAL FATHER?

Edmonds and Eidinow (2004) are quite confident that Regina never told Bobby about the identity of his real father. However, Nicholas (2009) presented some compelling evidence that Bobby likely knew that his biological father was Paul Nemenyi. First, he cited Eva Stallings, a long-time friend of Bobby's who was involved in trying to convince the German government to grant Bobby refugee status given his relationship to Hans Gerhardt Fischer, a German citizen. At one point Stallings showed Bobby a draft of a letter being submitted to the German government in which Hans Gerhardt was identified as Bobby's father. After reading the draft, Stallings reported to Nicholas (2009, p 1) that Bobby crossed out a passage that identified Gerhardt as his father, writing instead that Gerhardt was 'listed on my U.S. birth certificate as my father." Stallings believed that Bobby was signaling that his real father was someone other than Gerhardt.

A second source of evidence reported by Nicholas (2009) that leads me to believe that Bobby did indeed know the identity of his biological father, is the revelation of Zita Rajcsanyi, a Hungarian chess player and close friend of Bobby's, who incidentally is given the chief credit for enticing Bobby back to the chessboard in his rematch with Spassky in 1992 (see Brady, 2011; Polgar, 2005; Sneider, 2011). Rajcsanyi gave several interviews to Hungarian journalist and book author Tivadar Farkashazy (2008) in which she intimated that Bobby knew his father's identity. Specifically, Nicholas (2009) had relevant parts of Farkashzy's book translated and revealed the following:

> When Bobby was 9, Nemenyi disappeared from his life. It was only then that Bobby learned the truth, according to the book. He asked his mother why Nemenyi had stopped visiting, and she told him he had died. 'He was your father,' Regina told her son, according to Rajcsanyi. 'Didn't you know?' (pp. 4–5)

Whether Bobby knew the identity of his biological father early in his life we are not 100 percent sure. However, it is very likely, that he would have certainly known by the year 2002 when Nicholas and Benson's (2002) groundbreaking investigative report appeared in the *Philadelphia Inquirer* (he would have been 59 years of age). Given Bobby stayed up-to-date on chess topics reported in the media (see various interviews with Fischer insiders in Waitzkin, 1988), it is reasonable to assume that Bobby was aware of the *Philadelphia Inquirer* report or the well-reputed investigative text by Edmonds and Eidinow (2004). It is known that journalists Nicholas and Benson did attempt to make Bobby aware of their *Philadelphia Inquirer* stories and sent them by both FAX and Federal Express to his then girlfriend, Miyoko Watai, care of the Japanese Chess Association (Clea Benson, personal communication, September 12, 2011).

Suffice it to say, whether or when Bobby learned of his biological father's identity, would have implications for his own sense of identity and his psychological development. It is my perception that unexplored and unresolved father-son issues with both Bobby's biological father, Paul Nemenyi, and stepfather, Hans Gerhardt Fischer, contributed significantly to his psychological development beginning early in childhood and lasting until his death in 2008. We pick up on this topic in the next two chapters.

Chapter Six

THE MIND AND INNER LIFE
OF BOBBY FISCHER

To think of Bobby Fischer is to think of contradictions—purity and complexity, disarming innocence and shackling suspicion, consummate talent and tantalizing reluctance. He surpasses all in comprehending the chess pieces, but trails in understanding himself.

(Dr. Anthony Saidy, 1972, p. 151)

BOBBY'S PSYCHOLOGICAL PROFILE

Since early childhood Bobby was fiercely independent, eccentric, and lacked conventional social skills. The earliest recollection of Bobby's developing personality was presented in Brady's (1973) biography. Brady recounted the following story of Bobby wandering off on his own when living with his mother and sister in Mobile, Arizona:

> Early one afternoon, young Bobby strayed from the family environs and, after walking a while, suddenly grew tired. An independent and self-confident child, he sat down right where he was and began to play. There was only one trouble: in his naiveté the playground he choose was the cinder-supported tracks of the Southern Pacific Railroad. . . . He was discovered eventually by a frantic mother, and couldn't quite understand the reason for her excitement. (p. 2)

Though a child wandering off on his own is not uncommon, the story may portend Bobby's independent and unconventional path taken through his lifetime.

Though focusing primarily on Regina Fischer and the men in her life (namely Hans Gerhardt Fischer and Paul Felix Nemenyi) the FBI file (discussed at length in Chapters Four and Five) does include information collected on Bobby. At one point, FBI headquarters requested that agents try to discover why Bobby was upset and angry with his Soviet hosts while playing chess in the Soviet Union in 1958. During this investigation an FBI interviewee described Bobby as a very sick boy emotionally in such a mental state at the present time that losing an upcoming tournament (in Portoroz, Yugoslavia) may cause him to become violent and may cause him to be confined to a mental institution (FBI Report # NY 100–102290). Once again, we have to be cautious in interpreting FBI interviewee impressions. At this stage in Bobby's chess career he had lost a good number of chess games and appeared to adequately handle losing games; it is simply a fact of life in high level chess competition. However, a key point being made by this FBI interviewee and others in the FBI report is that Bobby was psychologically unstable and a number of people in his life were worried about his mental health.

Some insight into Regina Fischer's perceptions of her son Bobby's psychological and social challenges can be gleaned through her correspondence with her friend Joan Rodker, a retired journalist. The *Timesnow* gained access to unpublished letters written between Regina and Joan during the time period 1957 through 1960. In letters written to Joan from Regina, Mrs. Fischer lamented her poor relationship with her son Bobby. In a letter dated May, 1959, Regina wrote, "I have found I am not very necessary or useful to Bobby, and actually my presence is an irritant to him" (Quinn & Hamilton, 2008, p.1). Earlier, in a letter written in 1957 (Bobby would have been 14 years of age), Regina Fischer wrote to Mrs. Rodker, describing Bobby as "tempermental, unable to get along with others, without friends his age, and without any interest other than chess" (Quinn & Hamilton, 2008, p. 1).

Bobby's mother was not the only one to be concerned with Bobby's mental state in his youth. Nicholas and Benson (2003) describe a meeting held at the Marshall Chess Club in New York City in the late 1950s where Bobby's emotional stability was discussed by the club's Board of Governors. The source of information was Allen Kaufman, a New York Chess Master and childhood friend of Fischer's who was present at the meeting. Below is the meeting description:

At the Marshall Chess Club, no one doubted the teenager's talent. But his prickly behavior was alienating some of the wealthy sponsors whose support he would need to rise to the top. 'Some of what he did was so outrageous it was decided maybe he had emotional problems,' says Kaufman, who attended the meeting. What to do? Board members talked about finding a psychiatrist. They considered Reuben Fine, himself one of the giants of the game. Then someone raised a question: What if therapy worked? What if treatment sapped Fischer's drive to win, depriving the United States of its first homegrown world champ? Meeting adjourned. No one, Kaufman recalls, wanted to tamper with that finely tuned brain. (Nicholas & Benson, 2003, p. 4)

In discussing this scene with biographer Frank Brady (personal communication, July 13, 2010) who was active in the Marshall Chess Club during Bobby's involvement (and who is, incidentally, its current [year 2011] President), he noted that the conversation reported by Nicholas and Benson (2003) likely occurred, though not in a formal meeting agenda, as implied in Kaufman's recollection. Brady believed the conversation was less purposeful and more casual and informal. However, the topic of Bobby's mental health and whether intervention should be advocated did take place among the Marshall Chess Club leadership.

An interesting side note regarding Bobby's general health status revolves around his required military service physical examination around 1964 given his presumed 1-A ("Available for unrestricted military service") draft status at the time. Brady (1973) reported that as a result of the examination, Bobby "was rejected, for reasons that have never been made public" (p. 80). More recent investigative research by Brady (2011) has uncovered Bobby's draft card which listed him as classification 4-F, "Registrant not acceptable for military service." According to the U.S. Code of Federal Regulations in force in the 1960s (Title 32, Chapter XVI (Selective Service System), Section 1630, Classification Rules), a 4-F classification means that: "A registrant must have been found not qualified for service in the Armed Forces by a Military Entrance Processing Station (MEPS) under the established physical, mental, or moral standards."

To my knowledge, Bobby did not suffer from any physical ailments and he has always been described as somewhat athletic in terms of his interest and activities in swimming, skiing, skating, tennis, walking, and bowling (see Kasparov, 2003). Therefore, it may be possible that Bobby was rejected for service in the U.S. military due to psychological and personality factors. Another possibility is that the military was privy to the fact that Bobby's mother Regina, and his father (of birth certificate-record), Gerhardt Fischer were both under FBI investigation (see Nicholas, 2009), and therefore Bobby was rejected on national security grounds. Of the two options, the latter is more likely in that the psychological component of the physical exams were only cursory (asking about homosexuality and education levels), whereas during the cold war period the military had strong links with the FBI and other criminal/investigation units and Bobby's parents' surveillance status would have prevented Bobby's military induction (A. Audette, Colonel, United States Air Force [USAF], Retired, personal communication, July 27, 2010). Of course both of these hypotheses are just conjecture at this point, as the examination results have never been made public.

A number of chess grandmasters who spent time with Bobby and observed his behavior at various chess tournaments intimated or stated directly their perception that Bobby was psychologically deeply troubled. Although they are not trained mental health professionals, the opinions of some of these highly intelligent chess players are worth noting. Mikhail Tal mocked Bobby for being 'Cuckoo" at a tournament in Yugoslavia in 1958 (Bobby would have been about 15 years of age; see Solotaroff, 1992). Fischer's long-term biographer, Frank Brady, recently stated to me (personal communication, July 13, 2010) that Tal's mocking was likely done deliberately to rattle Bobby during tournament play, rather than to offer a serious opinion as to Bobby's mental state.[1]

In contrast to Tal's insulting (or joking) comment directed towards Bobby, Grandmasters Robert Byrne and Pal Benko were genuinely concerned with Bobby's mental state and suggested directly to him that he see a psychiatrist. More specifically, at a tournament in Bulgaria in 1962 (Bobby would have been approximately 19 years of age), Byrne suggested that Bobby see a psychiatrist, and Bobby replied that "A psychiatrist ought to pay him for the privilege of working on his brain" (Weber, 2008, p. A. 16). Benko stated that "I am not a psychiatrist, but it was obvious he was not normal . . . I told him, 'You are paranoid,' and he said that 'paranoids can be right'" (McClain, 2008, p. B10).

Benko's observation that Bobby exhibited paranoid tendencies supports similar observations recorded throughout Bobby's life, beginning in adolescence, and perhaps earlier. For example, in Bobby's often-cited interview with Ralph Ginzburg (1962), Fischer shared that he doesn't watch TV much as he is "a cautious person" and that he read somewhere that "every time you watch TV you get a little radiation" (p. 54).

After the interview Ginzburg took Fischer out to eat to "a posh expresso [sic] house," where the following exchange took place:

> Bobby ordered a slice of pecan cream pie, a side order of butter cookies, and an elaborate frozen pineapple drink. When he had finished his pie, I mentioned that the place was reputed to be owned and operated by homosexuals. Bobby was horrified and eyed the waiters narrowly. 'Gee, you'd think the place would die off with a reputation like that.' He turned his attention to his drink. 'Maybe they put something in here. I better not drink it.' He didn't touch it again. Nor did he eat any more of his cookies. (Ginzburg, 1962, p. 55)

I remind readers that Bobby denied making some of the statements attributed to him by Ginzburg (see detail in Chapter Four). However, despite Bobby's denials of statements made to Ginzburg, there is ample evidence of levels of paranoia that exceed normal ranges, even for celebrity status.

In his *New York Times* Obituary of Bobby Fischer, Weber (2008) noted that Bobby

> began making outlandish demands on tournament directors–for special lighting, special seating, special conditions to ensure quiet. He complained that opponents were trying to poison his food, that his hotel rooms were bugged, that Russians were colluding at tournaments and prearranging draws. He began to fear flying because he thought the Russians might hide booby traps on the plane. (p. A16)

In his book, *Searching for Bobby Fischer: The World of Chess, Observed by the Father of a Chess Prodigy* that was also made into a motion picture, Waitzkin (1988) interviewed a number of former close friends of Bobby Fischer. One friend, Ron Gross, knew Fischer in their youth in New

York City, and then became very close friends with him when they lived in California during the 1970s and 1980s. Gross shared with author Waitzkin the following memories of a fishing trip with Bobby to Ensenada, Mexico:

> He looked terrible . . . clothes all baggy, wearing old beat-up shoes. . . . Then I noticed that he was favoring his mouth, and he told me that he'd had some work done on his teeth; he'd had a dentist take all the fillings out of his mouth . . . I said "Bobby, that's going to ruin your teeth. Did you have him put plastic in the holes?' And he said, "I didn't have anything put in. I don't want anything artificial in my head.' He'd read about a guy wounded in World War II who had a metal plate in his head that was always picking up vibrations, maybe even radio transmissions. He said the same thing could happen from metal in your teeth. (Waitzkin, 1988, p. 200)

There is a continuity of anecdotal, observational data that Bobby had and shared thoughts indicative of some level of paranoia. However, in all fairness to Bobby, some of his suspicions were well warranted. For example, his suspicion that the Russian players were colluding by quickly drawing against each other to save their energy for non-Russian players, was recently proven to be true. More specifically, researchers Moul and Nye (2009) examined international qualifying tournaments from 1940 through 1998, and found that the probability of match results through fair open play to be only 25 percent; whereas the probability of the match results under the Soviet draw-collusion hypothesis was 60 percent. The scientific rigor in this study, employing statistical simulations, was exceptional and the results provide marked evidence for Soviet player draw-collusion. Bobby Fischer was correct: the Russians were cheating.

BOBBY FISCHER'S PSYCHOLOGICAL DETERIORATION

After winning the world chess championship in 1972, Bobby lapsed into a period of isolation and growing paranoia, manifested primarily in virulent and vitriolic anti-Semitism. These anti-Semitic (and anti-American) rants could be heard on various radio broadcasts Bobby made in the Philippines and Hungary. Of course, Bobby's mother

Regina Fischer was Jewish. Edmonds and Eidinow (2004) wondered whether some of the roots in Bobby's hatred of Jews stemmed from rejection of his mother. Importantly, Bobby's (likely) biological father, Paul Nemenyi, was also Jewish. Though Nemenyi supported Bobby financially, to some degree, for many years and visited him on occasion, he was obviously a distant and unavailable father figure. Bobby's parental situation is further complicated in that it appears Regina did not openly acknowledge that Nemenyi was Bobby's father. Nemenyi was kept secret in many ways. If Bobby knew early in life that Nemenyi was his "real" father, as some believe (Farkashazy, 2008; Nicholas, 2009), he may have been angered by his mother's secretiveness about Nemenyi, and he may have felt abandoned (and distrustful) of his father, who was Jewish.

In his new biography of Fischer, Brady (2011) cites an unnamed family relative who believes that Regina kept Bobby's true paternity a secret, and promoted the belief that Hans Gerhardt was the father, and listing him so on Bobby's birth certificate because "she didn't want Bobby to be known as a bastard" (p. 16). In addition to anger at his mom for being often unavailable given her long work hours, Bobby may have also felt angry believing that Regina kept his father away from the family. According to FBI Reports, Nemenyi told a Jewish Family Service worker that "he wanted the responsibility of maintaining the child and in 1947 he joined the subject [Regina Fischer] in Los Angeles, however, she assumed an attitude of hostility toward him" (FBI Report # NY 100–102290, p. 26).

This attitude of hostility, according to Nemenyi, motivated him to leave Los Angeles, and in fact in 1947 he left Regina and the family and travelled to Paris to attend a conference. In 1947, Bobby would have been about four years old, and perhaps old enough to sense the tension between his mother Regina and his likely father Paul Nemenyi. A number of friends and mentors of Bobby Fischer mentioned that Bobby could be upset for hours at the mere mention of his father (e.g., Brady, personal communication, February 8, 2011; see also Solotaroff, 1992).

Another association of "abandonment" with Jewishness may have occurred for young Bobby when the Fischer family settled into their Lincoln Place, Brooklyn address. Brady (2011) vividly describes the following kitchen-table scenes when Regina would invite her friends over for discussions:

At night and on weekends, there were often lively discussions around the kitchen table, sometimes with friends—mostly Jewish intellectuals. The subjects often revolved around politics, ideas, and cultural issues. Arguments over Palestine and Israel and the possibility that Eisenhower might run for president. (p. 14)

According to Brady (2011), both Joan and Bobby were present during these kitchen-table discussions and debates, and though Bobby heard the discussions, he never participated. Brady reported that years later Bobby said that he "hated" all that kind of intelligista discussion (p. 14). Thus we have a young child, perhaps feeling abandoned by his biological father, and now even his mom "abandons" him symbolically in that she spends some evenings with intellectual friends (many of whom were also Jewish) leaving Bobby to tend on his own or rely on big sister Joan for companionship. Perhaps a final felt sense of abandonment was when Regina, on her peace march from San Francisco to Moscow, met and eventually married Cyril Pustan (who also happened to be Jewish). In some illogical way to us, but logical to Bobby, he associates his deep feelings of hurt, betrayal, and abandonment with some notion of "Jewishness."

Also speaking to the topic of the origins of Bobby's anti-Semitism, Kasparov (2003) wondered whether Bobby's anti-Semitism was related to his conflicts with Jewish-American Grandmaster Samuel Reshevsky as well as his dislike of other Jews involved in the chess community, including wealthy sponsors (the Piatigorsky family), chess arbiters, and various journalists. Kasparov adds another interesting observation:

I think Fischer's anti-Semitism mania, which increased with the years, was largely associated with the domination of 'Soviet-Jewish' players. It seemed to him that they were all united against him with the aim of preventing him from becoming world champion. I remember Reshevsky telling me how, during the Interzonal tournament on Mallorca, with burning eyes Fischer informed him that he was reading a 'very interesting book.' 'What is it? Sammy asked innocently. *'Mein Kampf!'* Bobby replied. (Kasparov, 2003, p. 280–281)

Interestingly, in my recent conversation with Bobby's brother-in-law, Russell Targ, he also hypothesized that the roots of Bobby's anti-

Semitism stemmed from his adversarial relationship with Samuel Reshevsky. Bobby believed that money raised by chess organizations to support his chess ascendancy was diverted to Reshevsky (R. Targ, personal communication, July 20, 2010). Brady (personal communication, February 9, 2011) also noted that many in the leadership (including Directors) of the American Chess Foundation at the time were Jewish and Bobby felt the Foundation was giving more support to Reshevsky than to him, which was the case. Regardless of the origins of Bobby's unspeakable anti-Semitism, his anti-Jewish rantings, in time, alienated the majority of former friends, mentors, and supporters. There is a litany of individuals, couples, and families who once cared for or helped Bobby who eventually would cut relations with him. To be sure, some of these breaks were first initiated by Bobby due to a perceived (usually erroneously) slight or affront. Among those social supports that Bobby lost were Jack Collins, his chess teacher (after Carmine Nigro) for 15 years, and his sister Ethel (who was motherly towards Bobby); the Polgar and Lilienthal families who he visited and spent a good amount of time with in 1993 in Hungary, among many others (see Brady, 2011).

Bobby's long-time biographer, Dr. Frank Brady, who has always been fair and balanced in his profiles of Bobby (Brady, 1965, 1973, 2011) could no longer tolerate Bobby's vitriolic anti-Semitism. Soon after Bobby's death in 2008, Dr. Brady was interviewed by *New York Times* journalist Dylan Loeb McClain (2008, p. B10) and stated that Fischer's "Anti-Semitic and anti-American rants, particularly after the terrorist attacks of Sept. 11, 2001, were unacceptable. . . . It is something that I can never forgive." Even Bobby's own loving family could not tolerate his virulent anti-Semitism. Russell Targ reported to me that at one period in time when Bobby was living with Russell, Joan, and their three children, Joan and Russell asked him to move out as they did not want the children, particularly, exposed to Bobby's outspoken hatred of all things Jewish (R. Targ, personal communication, July 20, 2010).

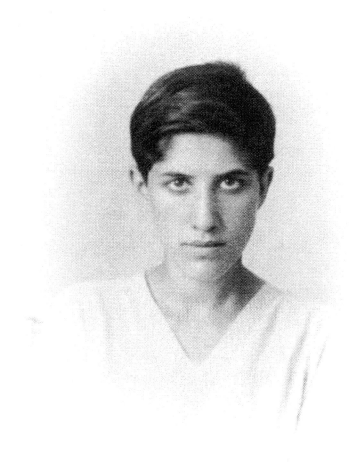

Plate 1. Regina Fischer as a young woman. One of the earliest photos of Regina Fischer; the facial similarity to son Bobby is evident. (Source: Russell Targ, from the Russell Targ Family Photo Archive, used with permission.)

Plate 2. Regina Fischer as a young woman. This photo and the previous one show Regina's beauty. She was extremely intelligent, highly educated; earning both M.D. and Ph.D. degrees, and was multilingual. (Source: Russell Targ, from the Russell Targ Family Photo Archive, used with permission.)

Plate 3. Regina and Hans Gerhardt Fischer, here we see Gerhardt and Regina in happier times; they are the parents of Joan Fischer, who would also figure prominently in Bobby's life. (Source: With permission from the Marshall Chess Club Foundation, New York City, and President Dr. Frank Brady.)

Plate 4. Regina Fischer with daughter, Joan, circa 1940. An obviously happy Joan with her mother. (Source: Russell Targ, from the Russell Targ Family Photo Archive.)

Plate 5. Paul Felix Nemenyi, young adulthood. The facial similarity to Bobby Fischer (see book cover) is evident. (Source: The California Institute of Technology Archives.)

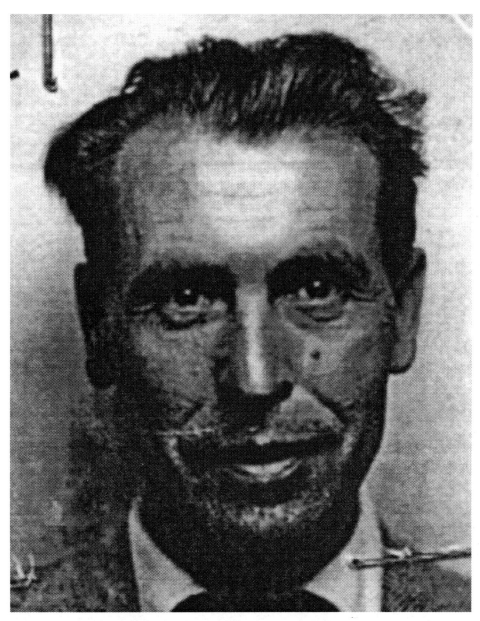

Plate 6. Paul Felix Nemenyi, middle adulthood. Again, the facial similarity to Bobby in older years (see Plate 9) is also evident. (Source: U.S. Citizenship application, U.S. State Department National Archives and Records Administration, in the public domain.)

Plate 7. Bobby Fischer with mentor Jack Collins. Here we see Bobby's lighthearted nature as he plays chess with his longtime mentor Jack Collins in Brooklyn. (Source: From Collinskids1912 at the Wikipedia project released into the public domain.)

Plate 8. Bobby Fischer with sister Joan Fischer. (Source: Photo by Richard Meek, from Sports Illustrated, with permission of Gettyimages.)

Plate 9. Last known portrait of Bobby Fischer taken by his Icelandic friend Einar Einarsson. (Source: Reprinted with permission of Einar S. Einarsson, photographer.)

BOBBY FISCHER - lead pencil drawing by Svala Soleyg after his last portrait by Einarsson

Plate 10. Bobby Fischer, lead pencil drawing by Svala Soleyg of the last known portrait of Bobby Fischer, taken by his Icelandic friend Einar Einarsson. (Source: Reprinted with permission of Einar S. Einarsson, photographer.)

Chapter Seven

A PSYCHOLOGICAL AUTOPSY
OF BOBBY FISCHER

In 1997 he despaired at the death of his mother, Regina, and then at the passing of his sister Joan, who first taught him the moves of the game. He began to sound increasingly insane, becoming angrier, louder, even exulting publicly when America was attacked on 9/11: 'Wonderful news,' he said.

(Nack, 2008, p. 1–2)

I am always on the attack.
    (Bobby Fischer to Frank Brady when asked about his approach to the game, cited from Brady, 2011, Marshall Chess Club Presentation)

Unfortunately, Bobby took this tremendous strength on the chessboard–"always on the attack"–off the board, into everyday life and became antagonistic to all. What made him great in chess hurt him in his life outside of chess–he could not compartmentalize attacks on the chessboard from attacks on people, friends, and systems (FIDE, U.S. Government, Jews). This chapter provides a detailed psychological autopsy of Bobby Fischer.

WHY CONDUCT A PSYCHOLOGICAL
AUTOPSY OF BOBBY FISCHER?

What is the purpose and value of conducting a more formal psychological autopsy of Bobby Fischer? For one, thousands of chess fans and many mental health professionals are curious to know what drove

Bobby to his isolation, paranoia, and rage–a rage directed at "former" friends who he felt betrayed his trust, rage at the Jewish people, rage at the United States, and his rage in general. Was Bobby a mean or evil person, or is there some psychological disorder and/or confluence of life events that could explicably lead to the "verbally violent" persona Bobby presented to the world? Bobby was a child prodigy, a chess genius; could he have been helped to lead a more balanced, healthy, and happy life? By studying Bobby's personal, family, and environmental history, perhaps parents, teachers, and mental health professionals will be in a better position to help other prodigies develop their genius, but also adjust and adapt to the broader society.

ON THE NATURE OF A PSYCHOLOGICAL AUTOPSY

A psychological autopsy

> is a process designed to assess a variety of factors including behavior, thoughts, feelings, and relationships of an individual who is deceased. In effect, it is a psychological evaluation conducted without benefit of direct observation but often with greater access to behavioral data about a person than a standard evaluation would provide. (Ebert, 1987, p. 52)

Ebert (1987) traces the origins of the psychological autopsy to the work of Shneidman (1969, 1973, 1981; Shneidman & Farberow, 1961) and noted that this procedure is applied in many contexts, with particular popularity in forensic evaluations to help determine the mode of death (e.g., accident, suicide, homicide) and the circumstances surrounding or leading to the death. The concept and tool of the psychological autopsy has been adeptly adapted for use by mental health professionals working on college campuses in suicide prevention efforts (Grieger & Greene, 1998).

Ebert (1987) developed a comprehensive set of 27 guidelines to consider in the psychological autopsy. In the present post-mortem examination of Bobby Fischer's mental status, a number of Ebert's guidelines apply, including a review of writings, relationship assessments, mood states, psychosocial stressors, language used, medical history, psychological history, family history, educational history, and police reports.

In the present chapter, the focus is not to understand the medical causes of Bobby's death, which have been reported to be natural causes due to kidney failure (Weber, 2008), but to understand his psychological functioning and mental health status throughout his life.

Diagnosing Bobby Fischer

I believe Bobby had some genetic vulnerability to develop a mental illness, and that this predisposition in concert with early life trauma and the burden of relentless media pressure, coalesced into serious mental health concerns that called for early and ongoing psychological intervention. Bobby Fischer was not a patient of mine, and I have not had access to any mental health records on Bobby, his sister Joan, or his mother Regina, save for those included in the 994-page FBI file on Regina Fischer that I secured through the Freedom of Information Act. As I emphasized in Chapter One of this book, it is inappropriate of me to proffer a formal psychological diagnosis of Bobby. Below I revisit the section of the ethical code of the American Psychological Association that relates to my post-mortem assessment:

> Psychologists provide opinions of the psychological characteristics of individuals only after they have conducted an examination of the individual adequate to support their statements or conclusions. When, despite reasonable efforts, such an examination is not practical, psychologists document the efforts they made and the result of those efforts, clarify the probable impact of their limited information on the reliability and validity of their opinions, and appropriately limit the nature and extent of their conclusions or recommendations. (APA, 2002, 9.01(b) Bases for Assessment, p. 13)

Therefore, the mental illness hypotheses presented below should be considered speculative, not validated, and in need of independent scrutiny from other mental health professionals who in time will have access to expanded archival documentation on the life of Bobby Fischer and his family. Furthermore, mental health professionals often rely on the *Diagnostic and Statistical Manual of Mental Disorders,* 4th edition, text revision (*DSM-IV-TR,* 2000) to cluster client symptomotology and arrive at specific diagnoses. Though a very useful classification tool in terms of promoting research and best-practice treatment, the *DSM-IV-*

TR is not without limitation (see, particularly Ivey & Ivey, 1998; Lopez et al., 2006; Zalaquett, Fuerth, Stein, Ivey, & Ivey, 2008). Chief among these limitations is that the *DSM* diagnostic process is categorical, arriving at diagnostic impressions based on the presence of select symptoms over specified periods of time. In actuality, understanding "normality" and "pathology" is more likely a dimensional process in that personality traits and behaviors are placed on a continuum, and where towards the center of the continuum the trait or behavior is considered within a "normal" range, and towards either end of the continuum, based on social and cultural context, the trait or behavior may be considered "pathological" (T. Millon, Grossman, C. Millon, Meagher, & Ramnath, 2004).

For example, a person may exhibit a certain degree of gregariousness, openness and talkativeness, that is generally considered within a normal range. However, if this cluster of adjectives were taken to either extreme, it might raise mental health concerns. More specifically, if the person exhibited too much of these characteristics given the social-cultural expectation and milieu, she or he might be considered manic. At the other end of the continuum, if the person exhibited too little of these characteristics for the social-cultural context, he or she might be considered depressed or anti-social.

Therefore, my clinical descriptions of Bobby Fischer must be considered with this cautious lens. Extreme behaviors (e.g., isolation, anti-Semitism, ongoing broken friendships) and personality traits (e.g., paranoia) may reach the label of "mental illness" when they cause distress within the person, or problems in the person's family, social, and career life. Thus as I diagnose Bobby Fischer in this section of the chapter, I want to be sensitive to the stigma associated with categorical labels, such as those in the *DSM-IV-TR*. Furthermore, as an international celebrity and world icon, Bobby faced outside pressures and expectations that were extreme relative to average celebrities.

A Comprehensive Mental Health Assessment of Bobby Fischer

A comprehensive mental health assessment should take into account Bobby's entire life, and not focus only on select events or periods in this life. An accurate evaluation should weigh Bobby's family history, his behavior across diverse contexts over his lifetime, and the sociocultural and political context of his time. Given recent research on genetic predispositions in vulnerability to mental illness, assessment should also consider the likely mental status of Bobby's biological parents, grandparents, and half-siblings. Therefore, let us begin with a closer mental health status look at Bobby's nuclear family.

Bobby's Biological Parents and Grandparents

There is little mental health information available on Bobby's [likely] biological father, Dr. Paul Nemenyi. It is known that he was highly intelligent, an established physicist and technical author, who at one point worked for a short time with Albert Einstein's son, Hans Albert Einstein, at the University of Iowa hydrology lab (Nicholas & Benson, 2003). However, Dr. Nemenyi had trouble adjusting to the United States, and at least a couple of his colleagues thought quite negatively of Dr. Nemenyi's character.

Journalists Nicholas and Benson (2003) uncovered documents and letters where Dr. Nemenyi was described as "an unstable and undesirable person" by a committee member of the Emergency Committee in Aid of Displaced Foreign Scholars, and as "a misfit" by fellow Hungarian immigrant, Dr. Theodore von Karman, a respected aeronautical scientist (p. 6). Perhaps less judgmental and more observational were the memories of Paul Nemenyi provided by Charlotte Truesdell, the wife of Paul's close colleague Clifford A. Truesdell who was interviewed by the Nicholas and Benson investigative team. She remembers that Paul used to carry soap around in his pockets and hated to touch door handles.

Thus, despite his great intellect, there is some indication that Dr. Paul Nemenyi exhibited odd and/or disturbing behavior. However, the information on Dr. Nemenyi is quite limited and the quotes from the two sources cited by Nicholas and Benson (2003) do not constitute marked evidence of mental disorder. In contrast to the available information on Dr. Nemenyi, the available anecdotal psychiatric evidence on Regina Fischer is more robust and reliable. As first revealed in Chapter Four, according to the FBI file on Regina Fischer she had been given a psychiatric diagnosis of "stilted (paranoid) personality, querulent [sic] but not psychotic" (FBI Report # CG: 100–27015).

This psychological assessment reflected the diagnostic category parlance of the mid-1940s and would be considered outdated today. Using the current revision of the *DSM-IV-TR* (American Psychiatric

Association, 2000), Regina Fischer may have been diagnosed with Paranoid Personality Disorder (PPD), a nonpsychotic disorder of personality. However, keep in mind that Regina had good reason to be suspicious as in fact, she was being investigated by the FBI for over two decades.

A final generational link to Bobby Fischer where some information is available relates to his grandmother, Natalie (Abramson) Wender (Regina's mother). Though virtually no information is publically available regarding her psychiatric diagnosis, we do know that she was institutionalized at New Jersey State Psychiatric Hospital from 1918 until 1921, the year of her death at the age of 37 years. The circumstances and cause for her hospitalization are unclear (refer back to Chapter Four for more discussion).

Information on personality dispositions and mental health status of Regina (Wender) Fischer, Paul Nemenyi, and Natalie Wender is important for the purpose of understanding Bobby's mental state because of heritability estimates for personality traits and disorders. I will discuss this more fully and with greater technical accuracy later in this chapter.

Bobby's Half-Siblings

Assuming Dr. Paul Nemenyi to be Bobby's biological father, Bobby had two half-siblings: his sister Joan (born to Regina Fischer and Hans Gerhardt Fischer), who was present off and on throughout Bobby's lifetime, and his half-brother Peter, who was born to Bobby's likely biological father Paul Nemenyi and his wife. From the investigative work of Nicholas and Benson (2002, 2003), it is clear that Peter knew Bobby was his half-brother (refer back to Chapter Five). Like his father Paul, Peter was a gifted intellectual who received a Ph.D. in Mathematics from Princeton and who authored a respected book on statistics. However, according to Nicholas and Benson (2003),

> Peter's end was unhappy. Sick with prostate cancer, he killed himself [in 2002]. He had been living alone in a Durham, N.C., apartment crammed with statistics papers. Friends say they often spotted him pushing a collection of shopping baskets around town, wearing oven mitts for gloves. (p. 7)

There is not enough evidence to be confident of Peter Nemenyi's mental state throughout his life. However, the evidence uncovered by Nicholas and Benson (2003) certainly raises concern as to his mental health at the end of his life.

A most significant figure in Bobby's life, in addition to his mother of course, was his older sister Joan. With Regina's constant financial struggles and ongoing need to work long hours, Joan took on extensive responsibility in caring for her younger brother Bobby. In some ways, Joan became Bobby's "surrogate mother" in addition to his big sister. Remember, Joan too, did not have a present father-figure as her biological father, Hans Gerhardt Fischer, never joined the Fischer family in the United States. The last time Joan had been with both her mom and dad together was in 1939 in Paris, where the family lived for a couple of years before Regina and Joan moved to the United States. As highlighted in Chapter Five, Hans Gerhardt never entered the United States.

My impression was that Joan was the central ballast of a family seesaw. On one end of the seesaw was Regina, who was under constant financial stress, often angry and protesting some cause or another, and simply exhausted from her work life and single-parenting duties. On the other end of the seesaw was Bobby, who was clearly a sensitive and at times difficult child, with few friends his own age, bouncing from school to school and who needed constant looking after. It does not take much imagination to envision and even feel the stress that young Joan must have been under. There is now a wide literature on the stress of siblings living with a special needs sister or brother (see integrative reviews in Caspi, 2011).

At one point the daily stress on Joan was too much to bear. According to FBI documents (NY 100–1–2290, p. 24), an agency worker of the Jewish Family Services reported that the stress on Joan in caring for Bobby became overwhelming, forcing Joan to leave the Fischer's apartment and be admitted to the "Pleasantville Cottage School, Pleasantville, New York, a cottage plan institution connected with the Jewish Family Service. She was released with favorable recommendations, and returned to live with her mother."

The FBI report does not specify how long Joan lived at Pleasantville Cottage School. Despite some early family and psychological challenges, Joan was a stable and successful person, and there is no indication that Joan developed any mental illness. Joan's husband, Russell Targ described her as "a woman of extraordinary intelligence and limitless resourcefulness. She demonstrated those abilities in everything she did" (Targ, 2008, p. 124). Dr. Anthony Saidy, a former close friend of Bobby's who knew Joan well, remarked to me recently that "Joan was a lovely and sensitive woman" (Dr. Anthony Saidy, personal communication, October 11, 2011). It was clear that Joan was as much as possible, a reliable and constant source of support for her brother Bobby.

Given her mother's possible psychological instability and eccentric behavior, and her brother's odd behavior beginning early in life, Joan likely felt a weighty burden in caring for both. It appears Bobby was as close to his big sister Joan as he could be, given his interpersonal difficulties, general mistrust of others, and his paranoid tendencies. According to Bobby Fischer's friend and fellow chess player Sam Sloan, who spent time with Bobby in Reykjavik, Joan attended the 1972 victory celebration called the "Ball of the Century" at Laugardalsholl Hall (the same venue where the match had been played). Sloan (2009) recalled that Joan had been purposely seated far from Bobby as at that time he was not interacting with his sister. However, according to the memory of Russell Targ (personal communication, September, 22, 2011), Joan's husband, Joan and Bobby were on good terms at the time of the victory celebration.

Despite Bobby distancing himself at times from his sister Joan and her family, he did always reconnect with his family. He appeared to respect and be somewhat close to his two nephews and niece, and as reported in Chapter Four, Bobby's niece Elisabeth Targ and her then boyfriend Robert Lipton, helped Bobby at times during his "wilderness" years in the Los Angeles area. Bobby also relied on his sister Joan after his 1992 rematch with Boris Spassky. Joan visited Bobby while he was living in Budapest (Targ, 2008). At Bobby's request she transported much of his 3.5 million dollar match winnings by train to Zurich, where she opened an account in his name at the Union Bank of Switzerland. Bobby felt safer with his money in Switzerland given his fugitive status (Brady, 2011).

It is my clinical intuition that Joan's death, coming only a year after their mother's passing, was a devastating loss to Bobby. Furthermore, Bobby's own grief process was further complicated as he could not attend his mother's (1997), sister's (1998), or niece's (2002) funerals for a very realistic fear that he would be arrested upon landing on U.S. soil for his 1992 violation of U.S. sanctions on business in Yugoslavia when he played his rematch with Spassky.

Starting Out: Bobby's Genetic Predispositions

Though Regina Fischer's diagnosis in the early 1940s of "stilted (paranoid) personality, querulent [sic] but not psychotic" (FBI Report # CG: 100-27015) has not been validated beyond the initial Chicago-based Municipal Psychiatric Institute's assessment, if we assume its accuracy, what would be her biological son's vulnerability to develop paranoid symptoms? Research in the fields of behavioral genetics and personality psychology indicate the heritability estimates for Paranoid Personality Disorder range from a low of .21 (21% shared variance; Coolidge, Thede, & Jang, 2001) to a high of .66 (66% shared variance; Kendler, Myers, Torgersen, Neale, & Reichborn-Kjennerud, 2007), with a number of estimates falling in between these numbers (e.g., Kendler et al., 2006 at 50% of shared variance).

In summary, based on a number of studies using varied assessments of paranoid personality disorder, such as psychopathology questionnaires or direct structured clinical interviews, the vulnerability of Bobby to inherit some of his mother's paranoid symptoms was modest. Interestingly, Bobby's sister Joan, to my knowledge, did not exhibit paranoid tendencies at any point in her life. According to the *DSM-IV-TR* (2000), Paranoid Personality Disorder (PPD) "appears to be more commonly diagnosed in males" (p. 692). Further, keep in mind that Joan and Bobby most likely had different biological fathers and therefore different genetic histories.

Differential Diagnosis of Bobby's Mental Status

Precisely diagnosing mental illness is a challenging process even when the mental health professional has ongoing contact with her or his patient or client. Even with clear symptom patterns, there is some subjective impressions that guide diagnosis. For example, the same symptom, or cluster of symptoms, may be characteristic of different mental disorders. Empirical research assessing the inter-rater reliability of independent clinicians diagnosing the same psychiatric patient profile shows accuracy rates that parallel those found in traditional nonpsychiatric medical diagnoses (Pies, 2007). More specifically, inter-rater agreement in psychiatric diagnoses have been reported to range from .64 (Way et al., 1998) to .82 for psychosis (Polanczyk et al., 2003), .83 across the four major diagnoses of major depression, bipolar disorder, panic disorder, and alcohol dependence (Pies, 2007), and .45 (Hesse & Thylstrup, 2008) to .62 (Zimmerman, 1994) for paranoid personality disorder.

Therefore, to diagnosis Bobby Fischer's mental health status without repeated clinical interviews with him directly, and absent archival medical and psychological records, constitutes a tenuous process at best, and therefore, I again caution that the diagnoses hypothesized below are based on limited information and should be considered exploratory and speculative.

In attempting to enhance the reliability and validity of a psychological assessment and diagnosis, clinicians form "differential diagnoses," that help to screen-in and screen-out potential "best-bet" diagnoses through a systematic decision-tree process. In hypothesizing Bobby's mental status, a differential diagnosis would include Paranoid Personality Disorder, Asperger's Disorder, Schizophrenia (Paranoid type), and Delusional Disorder. According to the *Diagnostic and Statistical Manual,* 4th edition, Text Revision (*DSM-IV-TR,* 2000), Paranoid Personality Disorder is in the class of personality disorders represented by "an enduring pattern of inner experience and behavior that deviates markedly from the expectations of the individual's culture, is pervasive and inflexible, has an onset in adolescence or early adulthood, is stable over time, and leads to distress or impairment" (p. 685).

Asperger's Disorder (also known as Asperger's Syndrome) is first diagnosed in infancy, childhood, or adolescence "and is characterized by severe and sustained impairment in social interactions and the development of restricted, repetitive patterns of behavior, interest, and activities" (p. 80). Schizophrenia (paranoid type) and Delusional Disorder are both psychotic disorders. Schizophrenia is diagnosed when two or more of the following symptoms are present for a significant portion of time during a one-month period: delusions, hallucinations, disorganized speech, grossly disorganized or catatonic behavior, and negative symptoms (e.g., the lack of normal affect). The paranoid type of Schizophrenia includes "the presence of prominent delusions or auditory hallucinations in the context of a relative preservation of cognitive functioning and affect" (*DSM-IV-TR,* 2000, p. 313).

By contrast, Delusional Disorder is characterized by "one or more nonbizarre delusions that persist for at least 1 month" (p. 323) and where the individual does not meet the criteria for schizophrenia. It is important to distinguish between bizarre delusions, which are more characteristic of schizophrenia, and nonbizarre delusions, which are defining characteristics of delusional disorder (Morrison, 2007). Bizarre delusions are clearly implausible and do not derive from ordinary life experiences. An example of a bizarre delusion is "a person's belief that a stranger has removed his or her internal organs and has replaced them with someone else's organs without leaving any wounds or scars" (*DSM-IV-TR,* 2000, p. 299). Examples of nonbizarre delusions might include the belief that one is under surveillance by the police, or that the Russians or some religious group is "out to get me."

Of the four potential diagnoses discussed above, it is fairly clear that Bobby Fischer did not suffer from schizophrenia. This diagnosis was attributed to Bobby by V. Krylov, a specialist in "psychophysiological rehabilitation of sportsmen" who had worked with Anatoly Karpov for two decades. According to Kasparov's (2003, p. 475) mini-biography of Fischer, Krylov examined correspondence and articles on Fischer to arrive at this diagnosis. In my view, however, though Bobby did appear to suffer from nonbizarre delusions (the Jews are out to destroy me; the Russians may shoot down my plane), he did not meet any other characteristic symptoms of schizophrenia. More specifically, there is no history of hallucinations, his speech was not disorganized, derailed, or incoherent, his behavior was not catatonic or grossly disorganized, and he did not appear to demonstrate negative symptoms (e.g., inability to experience emotions). Experiencing nonbizzare delusions is not sufficient for a diagnosis of schizophrenia, paranoid type (or any other type of schizophrenia).

The second diagnosis that I rule out is Asperger's Disorder (or Asperger's Syndrome). This disorder was attributed to Bobby by BBC journalist Eidinow (reported in Quinn & Hamilton, 2008). A diagnosis of Asperger's disorder requires at least two of the following four characteristics: (1) marked impairment in the use of multiple nonverbal behaviors (such as eye contact); (2) failure to develop age-appropriate peer relationships; (3) lack of spontaneous seeking to share en-

joyment, interests, or achievements with others; and (4) lack of social
and emotional reciprocity. In addition, an Asperger's diagnosis also
requires one of the following four characteristics related to restricted
repetitive and stereotyped patterns of behavior, interests, or activities:
(1) preoccupation with one of more stereotyped and restricted patterns
of interest that is abnormal either in intensity or focus (e.g., spinning
things); (2) inflexible adherence to specific and nonfunctional routines
or rituals; (3) repetitive, stereotyped motor mannerisms (e.g., hand
flapping); and (4) persistent preoccupation or absorption with parts of
objects (*DSM-IV-TR*, 2000; Morrison, 2006).

Though Bobby Fischer did meet some of the criteria for Asperger's
Disorder, for example, in the first category above he did fail to develop peer relationships appropriate to his developmental level, and he
appeared to lack social or emotional reciprocity, he did not clearly
meet at least one of the characteristics in symptom group two, based
on known evidence. More specifically, it has not been reported that he
exhibited restricted and stereotyped interests. Although he certainly
did have an intense interest in and preoccupation with chess, this is
common among many chess prodigies. He did not appear to exhibit
nonfunctional rituals, nor has it been reported that he exhibited repetitive and stereotyped motor mannerisms, and/or a preoccupation with
parts of objects. In summary, though Bobby Fischer met some of the
criteria for a diagnosis of Asperger's Disorder based on the extant evidence, he did not meet a sufficient number in all of the required categories to be confident of such a diagnosis.

Childhood symptoms of Asperger's overlap to some degree with
the symptoms of Paranoid Personality Disorder (PPD). More specifically, PPD

> may be first apparent in childhood and adolescence with solitariness,
> poor peer relationships, social anxiety, underachievement in school,
> hypersensitivity, peculiar thoughts and language, and idiosyncratic
> fantasies. These children may appear to be 'odd' or 'eccentric' and
> attract teasing. In clinical samples, this disorder appears to be more
> commonly diagnosed in males. (*DSM-IV-TR*, 2000, p. 692)

Diagnostic criteria for PPD include at least four of the following
seven symptom clusters: "(1) suspects, without sufficient basis, that
others are exploiting, harming, or deceiving him or her; (2) is preoc-

cupied with unjustified doubts about the loyalty or trustworthiness of friends or associates; (3) is reluctant to confide in others because of unwarranted fear that the information will be used maliciously against him or her; (4) reads hidden demeaning or threatening meanings in benign remarks or events; (5) persistently bears grudges, i.e., is unforgiving of insults, injuries, or slights; (6) perceives attacks on his or her character or reputation that are not apparent to others and is quick to react angrily or to counterattack; and (7) has recurrent suspicions, without justification, regarding fidelity of spouse or sexual partner" (*DSM-IV-TR*, 2000, p. 694).

From the available accumulated data on Bobby Fischer, it appears he meets six of the seven criteria. To my knowledge, there is no reported evidence of criteria #7, regarding spousal or sexual partner suspicion. Thus, of the three potential diagnoses under consideration, Schizophrenia, Asperger's Disorder, and Paranoid Personality Disorder (PPD), the evidence is strongest for the latter, PPD. A tentative diagnosis of PPD is also supported by the genetic link to his mother Regina, who was formally diagnosed with the disorder.

In addition to paranoid behavior, Bobby, in adulthood, clearly manifested nonbizzare delusions. Thus in addition to Paranoid Personality Disorder, we must also consider Delusional Disorder. The diagnostic criteria for Delusional Disorder include (1) nonbizzare delusions of at least one month's duration; (2) ruling out a diagnosis of Schizophrenia; (3) apart from the impact or ramifications of the delusion, functioning is not markedly impaired; (4) absence of long-term mood episodes concurrent to delusional period; and (5) the delusions are not caused by medical or substance use effects. From the available evidence it appears Bobby meets these criteria for delusional disorder.

Of the various subtypes of Delusional Disorder, Bobby would fit the Persecutory Type, in which

> the central theme of the delusion involves the person's belief that he or she is being conspired against, cheated, spied on, followed, poisoned or drugged, maliciously maligned, harassed, or obstructed in the pursuit of long-term goals. Small slights may be exaggerated and become the focus of a delusional system. The focus of the delusion is often on some injustice that must be remedied by legal action (querulous paranoia), and the affected person may engage in repeated attempts to obtain satisfaction by appeal to the courts and other gov-

ernment agencies. Individuals with persecutory delusions are often resentful and angry and may resort to violence against those they believe are hurting them. (*DSM-IV-TR,* 2000 p. 325)

The above paragraph appears to describe Bobby's later life with a high degree of accuracy. He did experience nonbizarre delusions that the Jews were out to destroy him, he was often involved in filing law suits (none of which he won), and he did turn violent on at least three documented occasions (see Appendix B).

A leading hypothesis in terms of the course of Bobby's mental illness is as follows: Bobby's family history, particularly his mother's and grandmother's possible mental illness, predisposed him to modest vulnerability to Paranoid Personality Disorder (PPD). The fact that Bobby was a "difficult" child temperamentally, coupled with the stress of having no father figure (and/or perhaps not even knowing who his real father was for a period of his youth), and being raised by a single mother experiencing financial hardships, added to Bobby's psychosocial stress and his vulnerability to develop symptoms of mental illness.

Bobby's stress levels and vulnerability were further magnified by his fame and celebrity status and its accompanying media pressure. Though some prodigies, whether their gift is in chess, art, music, or acting, can handle celebrity status and relentless media pressure, others succumb under the intense pressure. Television celebrity, Dick Cavett (2011) who was interviewed for the documentary, *Bobby Fischer Against the World,* shared that "fame is horrendous on the psyche of the young; it totally distorts their world." Also speaking to this issue is noted psychobiographer William Todd Schultz, an expert on the psychological consequences of fame, who stated that: "My sense is that some people are simply temperamentally unsuited to be famous. Their talents merit fame, but their personalities don't stand up to it. . . . [Fame] can be crazy-making for some. The psychological cost, for some, is too high" (Schultz, 2009, pp. 1–2).

And so may have been the case for Bobby Fischer. For certain, his chess genius and accomplishments merited fame, but his personality coupled with an unstable, loosely structured early home environment, was not suited to withstand the whirlwind of media pressure that would follow him until death. Interestingly, Bobby Fischer's brother-in-law, Russell Targ, who is now 78 years old, and who first met Bobby when the chess prodigy was 14 years old, shared with me his perception that the media pressure was in large part to blame for Bobby's psychological troubles (R. Targ, personal communication, July 20, 2010).

It appears that throughout childhood and adolescence, Bobby exhibited symptoms of Paranoid Personality Disorder (PPD). It is doubtful whether Drs. Harold Kline, Ariel Mengarini, or any other psychiatrist or psychologist diagnosed Bobby with this disorder, or treated him specifically for this or any other mental illness. It also does not appear that any psychotropic medication was ever prescribed to Bobby. Interestingly, though Bobby's mother Regina brought Bobby to the attention of mental health professionals, at least some elder chess masters and role models, though suspicious of Bobby's mental health status, failed to encourage treatment for fear that psychological/psychiatric intervention might interfere with his chess genius and career trajectory (that is, to be World Chess Champion) (see Nicholas & Benson, 2003).

As Bobby moved out of regular tournament play in the 1970s he further isolated himself and his paranoia intensified. In some ways the structure, demands, and focus of chess tournaments may have confined or contained his paranoid thoughts and behaviors. Without the structure and discipline of preparing for and playing in chess tournaments, Bobby felt lost, directionless. In his television appearance on the Johnny Carson show after his 1972 World Championship victory he shared a poignant reflection. At one point in the interview, Johnny Carson asked him if he felt different after the match, to which Bobby responded: "I woke up the day after it [the match] was over and felt different, like something was taken out of me." Perhaps chess was an anchor for his sanity and functioning, and without that anchor he was now more psychologically vulnerable than ever. Bobby's chess identity had fused with his personal identity, and when he abandoned competitive chess and thus his chess identity, he was lost.

The psychosocial stressors on Bobby Fischer continued and intensified in the 1980s, 1990s and beyond through his arrest and 2-day jailing in 1981 in Pasadena, California; his arrest warrant in 1992 issued by the U.S. State Department for violating U.S. sanctions restricting business with Yugoslavia (see Appendix B); the untimely loss of three close family members, mother Regina in 1997, sister Joan in 1998, and

niece Elisabeth in 2002; his two separate arrests in Japan–jailed for 18
days in 2000, and for 9 months in 2004; his struggle to find a safe
haven from U.S. arrest and a nation to accept him as a citizen (finally
found through full Icelandic citizenship in 2005). Collectively, these
intense psychosocial stressors, particularly the deaths of close family
members, contributed to his psychological vulnerability which may
have facilitated the development of nonbizzare, persecutory delusions
(delusional disorder) which now were superimposed on his possible
premorbid (pre-existing) Paranoid Personality Disorder. Figure 7.1 presented below, presents a Differential Diagnosis Flow Chart outlining a
hypothetical diagnosis (Differential Flow Chart adapted from *DSM-IV-
TR* [APA, 2000] and Morrison [2007]). Readers again are cautioned as

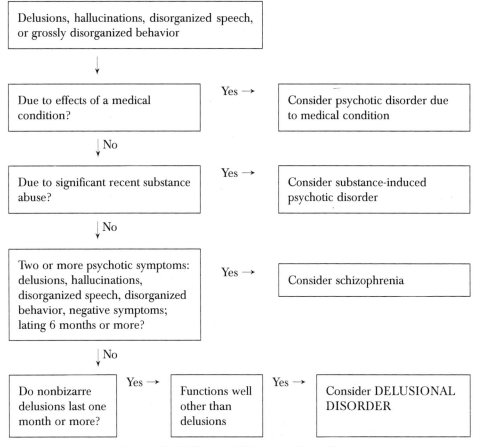

Figure 7.1. Differential Diagnosis Flow Chart.

to the tentative nature of any hypotheses regarding the mental state of Bobby Fisher.

The hypothesis of a delusional disorder in Bobby Fischer is further supported by limited research which shows that Paranoid Personality Disorder may be especially common among first-degree biological relatives of person's with Delusional Disorder (*DSM-IV-TR,* 2000). As we know, Bobby's mother Regina was formally diagnosed with Paranoid Personality Disorder in Chicago's Municipal Psychiatric Institute. Furthermore, Bobby's maternal grandmother, Natalie Wender, was a long-term patient at the New Jersey State Psychiatric Hospital at Greystone.

Morrison (2006) noted that the onset of Delusional Disorder is often later in life. Morrison also highlighted that individuals with Delusional Disorder can appear quite normal, as long as one does not bring up a topic related to their delusional theme. In fact, numerous former friends of Bobby's noted that he was pleasant to be with and talk with as long as the topic of Jews did not come up. His former close friend Shernaz Kennedy (personal communication, April 8, 2011), the Polgar sisters (Polgar, 2005), Ron Gross (Franett, 2000), and many other former acquaintances of Bobby's have made this point (see Waitzkin, 1988 for summaries of some interviews). Finally, individuals suffering from Delusional Disorder "are often swept up in litigation" (Morrison, 2006, p. 169), and Bobby was often suing individuals throughout his adulthood.

Chapter Eight

THE PARALLEL LIVES AND
MENTAL ILLNESSES OF PAUL
MORPHY AND BOBBY FISCHER

Paul Morphy: The Pride and Sorrow of Chess
(Spens, 1882)

Bobby Fischer: The Hope and Despair of Chess
(Ponterotto, this text)

Though most North Americans know the story of Bobby Fischer, few know the story of Paul Morphy; yet the stories of Fischer and Morphy bear a striking resemblance in many respects. Both were child prodigies who learned the game around six years old and became very good a few years later; both returned from chess victories abroad to a celebratory welcome, instant fame, and almost hero-like worship; both reached the exalted status of (officially or unofficially) World Chess Champion in their 20s; both left competitive chess at the pinnacle of their brilliance; and both developed symptoms of paranoia and delusions, and ultimately died in relative seclusion.

The purpose of this chapter is to compare and contrast the lives and psychological profiles of Paul Morphy and Bobby Fischer, the United States' two most renowned and revered chess personalities. Though playing a century apart, both world champions had similar earthquake-like impacts on the status and popularity of chess in the United States and world-wide. I begin the chapter with a brief reminder of the momentous impact both Morphy and Fischer had on the status of chess. I then present a biographical sketch of Paul Morphy for the reader who may be less familiar with his life and career. In order to accurately compare and contrast the lives and personalities of Morphy and Fischer, it is important to present the context and framework of Morphy's life much like was done for Bobby Fischer in earlier chapters.

ROCKING THE CHESS WORLD

> Both Morphy and Fischer shook the world of chess to its foundations with their games, their personalities, and their genius.
>
> (Lawson, 2010, p. 380)

Morphy's victory over European Champion Adolf Anderssen in Paris in 1858 ignited a nationwide interest in chess throughout the United States not to be seen again until Fischer's victory over Spassky in 1972. While the two stars were playing, chess fever and passion was at its zenith, and when the two players abandoned the game, the country's passion for chess subsided. The impact of Morphy on the status of U.S. Chess in the middle of the nineteenth century is captured in the "shooting star" parallel highlighted below in a January 27, 1861 article in *Wilkes's Spirit of the Times:*

> The Chess-mania which seized upon the whole nation when Morphy's brilliant star first rose on the horizon, was violent and exaggerated; and as his star rushed up into the zenith of its worldwide renown, and then with equal rapidity withdrew itself from the public gaze in the obscurity of private life, from which there seems small prospect of its reappearance, the fever died away with it, and it is not to be wondered at that Chess Clubs and Chess Columns, that owed their existence to the excitement of the day, should dwindle away and disappear. (cited in Lawson, 2010, p. 274)

The *Wilkes* article also noted that the context of the time, namely the "Southern rebellion" that led to the Civil War (begun in 1861), also figured prominently in dwindling interest in chess after Morphy's retirement from the game. Fischer's impact on the interest and popularity in chess after his championship victory and then retirement from tournament/match level play paralleled that of Morphy's. The geopolitical context for the ending of Fischer's active chess career was another war, the Vietnam war, which occupied center stage in the early 1970s.

Certainly the game of chess lived on after Morphy's and Fischer's retreat from the game, as there have been many exciting U.S. champions and national tournaments in the last century, but it is fair to say that absent Morphy's and Fischer's active involvement in chess, the game lost its broad-based appeal and "national obsession" status. Thus as Lawson's (2010) popular characterization of Morphy as "The Pride and Sorrow of Chess"[1] is apropos, so too is the depiction of Fischer as "The Hope and Despair of Chess."

The mental health/illness of Paul Morphy and Bobby Fischer was already being linked when Fischer was only 13 years old. More specifically, in 1956 when Dr. Reuben Fine, an International Grandmaster and renowned psychoanalyst, was in England meeting with the eminent psychoanalyst Dr. Ernest Jones, who had penned a psychoanalytic assessment of Paul Morphy (Jones, 1951), the two discussed Fischer. As Fine shared some of his psychological observations of Bobby Fischer, Jones predicted that Bobby Fischer's emotional life was headed for trouble, and opined to Fine, "Leave him alone; he'll become a second Paul Morphy" (Fine, 2008, p. 25). Indeed, in many ways, the latter years of Bobby's life were eerily similar to those of Paul Morphy.

THE LIFE OF PAUL MORPHY

This section reviews the life of Paul Morphy and provides a general outline of his family history, academic training, career pursuits, life in chess, and his psychological history. The summary provided here is integrated from various Morphy biographies (Buck, 1902; Edge, 1859; Lawson, 2010; Morphy-Voitier, 1926; Sergeant, 1957) and biographical sketches (Kurtz, 1993), but I rely particularly on Lawson's (2010) classic biography which I and others (e.g., Aiello, 2010) consider the definitive and most accurate record of Morphy's life. To supplement this text I provide a more detailed chronological time-line of critical life events for Morphy in Appendix D. I recommend to readers that they read this section and Appendix D side-by-side.

Family Origins and Early History

Paul Charles Morphy was born to a very prominent New Orleans family on June 22, 1837. He was the third of four children born to Alonzo and Thelcide Morphy. Paul had an older brother, Edward, an older sister Malvena, and a younger sister, Helena. Paul's father, Alonzo Morphy was of Irish heritage, his great grandfather changing his name from Michael Murphy to Morphy upon arriving in Spain from Ireland in 1753. Michael Morphy became a captain of the Royal Guard in Madrid, Spain before moving to Malaga where he became a successful merchant and then American consul at Malaga.

Michael Morphy married Maria Porro, Paul's great grandmother, who in 1765 gave birth to Diego, Paul's grandfather. Diego Morphy married his first wife Millie (Maria) Creagh, also of Irish descent, in 1789, and they had three children before her death in 1796. By this time the Morphy family had settled in Charleston, South Carolina. In 1797, Diego married his second wife, Louisa Peire, who bore five children while living in Charleston. The elder son, Alonzo, Paul Morphy's father, was born in 1798, and Alonzo's brother, Ernest was born in 1807. Ernest, who became one of New Orleans's best chess players, would figure very prominently in Paul's chess career, and was in fact the family's strongest supporter and promoter of his chess talents and promise (Sergeant, 1957).

In 1809, the Morphy family moved to Louisiana where Diego was appointed Spanish consul for the port of New Orleans. Paul's father, Alonzo Morphy, who was eleven years old when the family relocated to New Orleans became a lawyer, and by 1829 had risen to the honored post of Attorney General for Louisiana. Alonzo married Louise Therese Felicitie Thelcide Le Carpentier (commonly referred to as simply Thelcide or Telcide), an accomplished pianist, harpist, composer, and mezzo-soprano, in February of 1829. All the Morphy children were born at the family home on 1113 Chartres Street, moving to the (now famous) address of 89 Royal Street when Paul was four years old (Lawson, 2010).

Figure 8.1 to follow presents a family tree of the Morphy family. The family tree includes key figures in both Paul Morphy's maternal and paternal branches. When dates of birth or death could be confirmed, they are included as well. It is evident that Paul Morphy grew up in a privileged, "royal" family of means, quite in contrast to young Bobby Fischer.

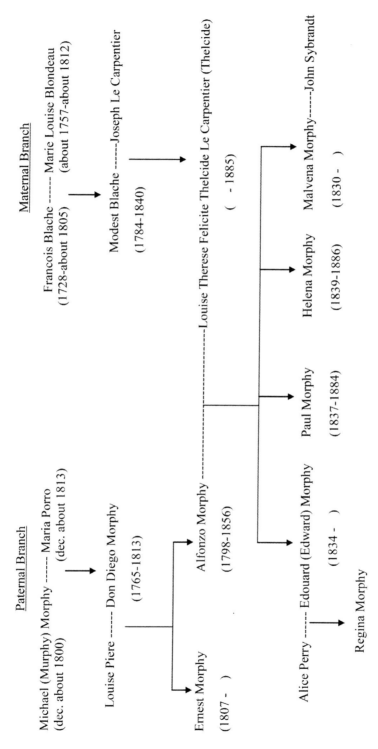

Figure 8.1. Paul Morphy Family Tree.

An Intellectual and Artistic Prodigy

In terms of academic ability, Paul was simply brilliant, and was a dedicated and focused student from early childhood. His early formal schooling was at the highly regarded Jefferson Academy in New Orleans. Charles Maurian, Paul's lifelong friend and classmate at Jefferson Academy reflected on Paul's early academic years in a 1909 issue of the *New Orleans Picayune:*

> A dreamy-eyed delicate boy, sitting at his little desk, his elbows on the boards, and his palms supporting chin, plunged in deep thought. Morphy was always thinking, thinking, thinking and there was a depth in his dark soulful eyes that it was hard to fathom. . . . Paul at school was always studious. . . . He preferred literature, but had a good head for mathematics [and] found enjoyment on sitting down with one of the classics. . . . Often when the boys were at their rough games in the courtyard Paul, not physically strong enough to join the pastime, would sit watching them with just the suggestion of longing in his eyes. . . . Paul's delicate physique was an early concern of his father, and with the hope of developing the lad, Judge Morphy engaged a famous maitre d'arms to instruct him in the art of fencing. Paul devoted himself to the exercise with the same application that he gave to everything else, and was soon quite a swordsman, but in after [later] years he dropped fencing entirely. (cited in Lawson, 2010, pp. 33–34)

It was during his years as a Jefferson academy pupil that Paul began playing chess. According to his friend Charles Maurian and his uncle Ernest Morphy, Paul learned the game of chess by watching elder family members play. His father Alonzo Morphy, his older brother Edward, his uncles Ernest Morphy and Charles Le Carpentier, and his maternal grandfather Joseph Le Carpentier all played chess. Lawson (2010) estimated that Paul began observing his father's chess games as a young boy, probably earlier than six years of age.

It is important to note that chess playing in the Morphy family was considered only a relaxing diversion from real life pursuits, namely academic and career development. In no way was it culturally acceptable to play chess full-time. Paul's father Alonzo and uncle Ernest often played on Sunday afternoons on the back porch of the Morphy mansion. According to Ernest Morphy, Paul was allowed to play chess only on Sunday afternoons and only for three of four games (Sergeant, 1957). Though chess was considered a valued intellectual career during Bobby Fischer's time, this was not the case in the elite society of New Orleans in the mid-1880s.

The earliest reported incident of Paul engaging the chessboard was described by Charles Maurian, Paul's lifelong friend. Apparently Paul was watching his father and uncle play one Sunday afternoon, and after a long game ended in an agreed-upon draw and the remaining pieces removed in preparation for a new game, Paul remarked to his uncle that he should have won the game. At first, Paul's father and uncle dismissed the boy's comments, asking him what would he know about the game? The actual scene at the chessboard was described by Maurian some 65 years after the incident in a 1909 article in the *New Orleans Picayune* newspaper; it unfolded this way:

> Paul, with the assurance of a born genius, asked leave to set the pieces in the final position, and just to humor him, his father consented. The boy faithfully and accurately arranged the men, and then studying the board only for a moment leaned forward and said: 'Here it is: check with the Rook, now the King has to take it and the rest is easy.' And sure enough it was. The child had seen a mate in an apparently impossible position, and the Judge and his brother simply stared at him, hardly able to express themselves in words. (cited in Lawson, 2010, p. 12)

It is uncertain how accurate Maurian's recollection of the event was so many years after the incident took place, but leading Morphy biographer David Lawson (2010) appears to give it reasonable credence. It is also not clear exactly how old Paul was when this incident took place, but it was certainly before he was eight years old, and very possible only six or seven years of age (see chronological analysis in Lawson, 2010).

It is documented that at the age of nine years old, Paul Morphy played his first publicly witnessed game against General Winfield Scott, a good amateur player, who had stopped in New Orleans for five days in December of 1846 on his way to Mexico to take command of the American Army. General Scott and young Morphy played two games in succession, with Morphy winning both games easily and quickly (Kurtz, 1993; Lawson, 2010). Apparently, General Scott was both stunned and embarrassed at his quick and resounding defeat at the hands of young Morphy. Kurtz (1993) writing on Paul Morphy in the journal, *Louisiana History: The Journal of the Louisiana Historical Association,* noted: "Flustered by the two defeats, Scott rose from the table and indignantly left the room without even congratulating the child" (p. 177).

Paul Morphy's developing competence and mastery of the game was chronicled by his niece Regina Morphy (daughter of his brother Edward), who penned a 40-page booklet on Paul titled *Paul Morphy in the Vieux Carre of New Orleans and Abroad* (Morphy-Voiter, 1926). Regina Morphy recalled that by the age of ten, Paul was winning games regularly against older and more experienced players. Furthermore, Morphy loyal friend Charles Maurian recalled that "it was a well known fact that Paul was a chess genius when he was barely nine years old" (cited in Lawson, 2010, p. 11).

In the few years following his defeat of General Winfield Scott, Paul's dominance over the New Orleans chess scene became more solidified. In 1849, Morphy defeated Frenchman Eugene Rousseau, who was then living in New Orleans and considered the city's best player. The next year, Paul soundly defeated the Hungarian political refugee Johann J. Lowenthal (a renowned chess player throughout Europe) who was visiting New Orleans. After his defeats of both Rousseau and Lowenthal, young Morphy's status as Louisiana's best chess player was unquestioned. Furthermore, thanks to letters written by Paul's uncle Ernest and sent to various newspapers and chess periodicals in the United States and Europe, Paul's prodigious chess talent became a topic of discussion far beyond the confines of Louisiana.

Young Paul was likely receiving contradictory messages about his chess prowess. On the one hand, his chess skill was a source of pride to the family, especially for his uncle Ernest, the family's biggest chess enthusiast. As a physically slight, timid boy with an older brother and a "strong" father figure, chess was a means for Paul to prove himself and establish his individuality within the family. On the other hand, chess was not considered a "legitimate" academic or career pursuit, so Paul's talent may not have been taken all that seriously by his parents.

While young Paul was beating New Orleans's best chess players, he was also finishing up his studies at Jefferson Academy. In 1850, at the age of thirteen, Paul graduated the Academy and left for Spring

Hill College (referred to as St. Joseph's College at Spring Hill by Sergeant, 1957) in Mobile, Alabama. Spring Hill College was a highly
respected Catholic institution of higher learning, and certainly it was a
source of pride for the Morphy family that first, Edward, and now Paul
were enrolled there. Spring Hill is Alabama's oldest institution and
was founded in 1830 by Michal Portier, Mobile's first Catholic
Bishop.[2] Spring Hill is also the third oldest Jesuit college and the fifth
oldest Catholic college in the United States.

Life in College and Law School

At Spring Hill College, Paul excelled in all academic subjects.
Lawson (2010) uncovered college records indicating that Paul's "conduct was excellent, application very earnest and unremitting and
improvement very rapid" (p. 34). He was proficient in literature, math,
science, music, the arts, and was multilingual with marked competence in Latin, Greek, French, Spanish, German, and English (Lawson,
2010; Sergeant, 1957).[3]

In addition to his academic brilliance, Paul was a good public
speaker and actor. He was elected President of the Thespian society in
his freshman year, and acted regularly in the school plays. For example, in 1851 he played the role of Charles in the Comedie Francaise,
Gregoire; and in 1852 he played the role of Portia in *The Merchant of
Venice.* Paul received his Bachelor of Arts (A.B.) Degree in 1854 and his
Master of Arts (A.M.) in 1855, at the ages of seventeen and eighteen,
respectively. In his A.B. thesis, written seven years before the Civil
War was to begin, Morphy argued against the use of forcible secession
in political upheaval. As will be discussed later in this chapter, Paul's
divided loyalties regarding the "Southern Rebellion" may have had a
negative impact a decade later in his attempt to start a law practice
after the Civil War (Lawson, 2010).

Of note is that during his years at Spring Hill College, Paul played
very little chess. The Morphy family long-held position that chess was
to be only an occasional avocation not to interfere with serious study
or career pursuits, apparently was ingrained in Paul. His best friend at
Spring Hill College, Charles Maurian, recounted a few incidences
where Paul would play against him and other friends, usually at strong
odds (removing one of his major pieces before play began). Furthermore, during his annual vacations back home in New Orleans, Paul

would again play some chess. But in marked contrast to Bobby Fischer who played chess consistently and constantly during adolescence, Morphy was relatively absent from the game.

After receiving his A.M. degree from Spring Hill College, Paul immediately enrolled in law school at the University of Louisiana. Two years later, on April 7, 1857, at the age of twenty, he was awarded his law degree (L.L.B.). Paul excelled in his law studies, as he had earlier in his academic studies at Spring Hill College and Jefferson Academy. With regard to his knowledge of the law, Lawson (2010) stated that "Blessed with an unusual memory, Morphy could easily recite by heart nearly the entire Civil Code of Louisiana" (p. 41). Knowing well the rigorous research methods and pin-point writing of Lawson, I believe this quote is not an exaggeration. The Louisiana historian Kurtz (1993) noted that Morphy could also cite from memory the entire Civil Code in French. Interestingly, in addition to perhaps a photographic memory, Paul apparently also had exceptional aural memory in that he could whistle the score of a full opera after hearing it the first time (Morphy-Voitier, 1926). Given his youth at graduation from law school, Paul had to wait a year to be admitted to the Louisiana Bar (minimum age, 21 years).

Embarking on his Brief Chess Career

While waiting a year to be of legal age to sit for the Louisiana Bar and then embark on his law career, Paul Morphy used the time to play serious competitive chess. In September of 1857, he agreed to participate in the Grand Tournament at the First Congress of the American National Chess Association to begin in October in New York. Paul's father's untimely death in 1856 caused him to initially decline to play in the Grand Tournament due to respecting the grief process, but in time and with the support of the New Orleans community he eventually decided to play (Lawson, 2010).

At the New York tournament, Morphy easily dominated the strong field of national players and becomes the first U.S. National Chess Champion. His strongest competition was with Louis Paulsen whom he defeated in the final championship match with eight wins, one loss, and three draws (Lawson, 2010). With an air of confidence Paul felt ready to challenge the strongest players in the world, and in 1858 he departed for England and France where he hoped to challenge Europe's top chess masters, particularly Howard Staunton, the English Champion. In the mid-1800s, Europe, particularly England and France, was considered the capital of the chess world where the best players competed. A century later during Fischer's career, Russia was the epicenter of chess brilliance.

Arriving in England in June of 1858 Paul Morphy did not appear, in the physical sense, to be the formidable and overpowering chess opponent he apparently was on the intellectual plain. Frederick Edge, his personal secretary and first biographer, who accompanied him on his European adventure described him as a "boy of twenty-one, five feet four inches in height, of slim figure, and face like a young girl in her teens. . ." (cited in Lawson, 2010, p. 205). A more detailed description of Morphy in June of 1858 was provided by Falkbeer for the German newspaper, *Deutsche Illustrierte Zeitung:*

> His image is vividly recalled to my memory as I first made his acquaintance in London in 1858. Of slight figure, below middle height, with fresh and youthful features delicately shaded by the first dawn of an incipient moustache, always plainly dressed, he appeared much younger than he really was. One would certainly have taken him rather for a schoolboy on his vacation than for a chess adept who had crossed the Atlantic for the express purpose of defeating, one after another, the most eminent players the world then knew. (cited in Sergeant, 1957, p. 33)

While in Europe, Paul defeated all challengers in quite a convincing manner, though he never engaged in match play against Howard Staunton. By most accounts, it appeared Staunton actively avoided and evaded a match with Morphy (Lawson, 2010; Sergeant, 1957). Morphy worked hard to try to arrange a match with Staunton, and the English champion's refusal to play was a source of great frustration for Morphy and his chess fans. However, in December of 1858, Morphy defeated European Champion, Adolf Anderssen, the winner of the famed 1851 European tournament, and was therefore hailed as Chess Champion of the World.

After defeating all European challengers and reaching his chess goals (save for playing and defeating Staunton), Morphy appeared ready to retire from competitive chess. More specifically, on January 5, Frederick Edge, Morphy's secretary, sent a dispatch to the *New York*

Herald relaying the news of Morphy's victory over Anderssen and announcing: "Paul Morphy had declared that he will play no more matches with anyone unless accepting Pawn and move from him" (cited in Lawson, 2010, p. 183). This pronouncement, which Morphy generally adhered to for the remainder of his life, effectively removed him from championship level chess matches, as serious contenders to the title would naturally want to play and beat Morphy on even terms.

The reasons for Morphy's essential abandonment of competitive chess at this time can only be surmised. Perhaps, given his socialization into the Morphy family and the elite class of New Orleans society in the mid-1800s where chess was frowned upon as an activity save for a Sunday afternoon diversion, Paul's pronouncement may have been a way of saying, "I will play chess occasionally with friends at odds, but now it is time for me to pursue the serious profession of law for which I was rigorously trained." Such a stance would allow him to play chess without media pressure, and would put him in the good graces of New Orleans's upper crust as now he is a serious "attorney at law," following in his father's footsteps and honoring the Morphy family legacy. Charles Maurian's obituary of his best friend published in the *New Orleans Times-Democrat* addressed his perception of the place of chess in Paul's life. He noted:

> Paul Morphy was never so passionately fond, so inordinately devoted to chess as is generally believed. . . . His only devotion to the game, if it may be so termed, lay in his ambition to meet and defeat the best players and great masters of this country and of Europe. . . . But, this one ambition satisfied, he appeared to have lost all interest in the game. (Sergeant, 1957, p. 34)

The Civil War and Life as an Attorney in New Orleans

Writing publicly against the notion of "forcible secession" as a cause for war, as Morphy did in his Bachelor's Degree thesis at Spring Hill College in 1854, would not have been a popular stance in New Orleans on January 26, 1861 when Louisiana became the sixth state to vote for secession from the Union. Lawson (2010) believed that Morphy had torn loyalties given his love for Louisiana and the south coupled with his anti-war stance as a rationale for secession. Perhaps in an attempt to express and demonstrate his loyalty to the south (his older brother Edward had joined the Seventh Regiment of New Orleans), Morphy traveled to Richmond, Virginia in October of 1861 to meet with General P.G.T. Beauregard, a family friend, to see if perhaps he could help the confederacy in a noncombative role. There is some debate whether Morphy actually served on Beauregard's staff in Richmond, but Lawson (2010) concluded that the General, finding Paul "was not war material" on or off the battlefield, convinced him to pursue other life courses (see also Buck, 1902). Thus after about a year living in Richmond (where he did play some chess for fun at "knight odds" [removing his knight before play began]), Paul (accompanied by Charles Maurian) left for Paris, France where his mother and sister Helena were waiting out the war. Paul remained in Paris until January, 1864, arriving back in New Orleans in February of 1864 after a week stopover in Havana, Cuba.

Upon his return from Paris and as the Civil War came to an end, Paul Morphy labored to open his law practice, but he failed to make a go at it. Buck (1902) and Lawson (2010) hypothesized that Morphy's reputation as the world's greatest chess player may have hindered the public taking him seriously as an attorney. Apparently, his notoriety only as a chess champion may have hindered him on the romantic front given chess was not considered a respectable career in the upper class of New Orleans. Buck (1902) recounted the following incident: [Morphy] became enamored of a wealthy and handsome young lady in New Orleans and informed a mutual friend of the fact, who broached the subject to the lady, but she scorned the idea of marrying a 'mere chess player'" (Buck, 1902, p. 21).

It is difficult to assess the accuracy of the story cited above as Buck's (1902) biography is poorly documented. In fact Lawson identified 16 blatant inaccuracies in Buck's biography (Lawson, 2010, pp. 226–227), and readers are cautioned to seek confirmation sources, as I did, before relying on Buck's memories or interpretations.

Other speculation is that since Morphy was widely known in New Orleans to have been against forcible secession (as noted in his A.B. Thesis at Spring Hill College), the deeply loyal southerners distrusted him to some degree.[4] A third conjecture not presented in Lawson is that back in New Orleans and no longer engaged in competitive chess, Morphy's mental health decline may have begun, which would naturally have hindered his ability to secure and retain a law practice clientele. Regardless of the reasons for Morphy's lack of success in a law career in Louisiana, it should be noted that Louisiana state law was rather unique relative to other states in the union and was heavily influenced by Napoleonic Code, and as a result it was not feasible for Morphy to attempt a law career outside of Louisiana. Though Morphy's chess brilliance and skills transcended states, his law skill was specific to Louisiana (Aiello, 2011, personal communication). It is also not clear whether Paul would have felt free to live and work in another state given family pressure and dynamics.

Psychological Decline and Death

By 1867, Paul's mother Thelcide noticed her son's increasing melancholy and social withdrawal, and in an attempt to alter this mental state persuaded Paul to sojourn in Paris with herself and Paul's sister Helena (Sergeant, 1957). It appeared that Paul's earlier 1858–1859 stay in Europe had been a positive and happy one, and his mother thought another long sojourn would do him well psychologically. After his third stay in Paris, this time for 15 months, Paul returned to New Orleans. Back home, Paul's emotional well-being continued to deteriorate and in 1875 he was brought by his mother, his best friend Charles Maurian, and his brother Edward to the "Louisiana Retreat," an institution for the mentally ill run by Catholic nuns (Buck, 1902; Sergeant, 1957). Paul refused admittance, clearly citing the rule of law on his behalf, and was returned home. Unfortunately, from 1875 up until his death, reports of Morphy's paranoid ideation and delusions appeared with increasing frequency.

The chief persecutory delusion experienced by Morphy was that his brother-in-law John Sybrandt, who was married to his older sister Malvena and who was the executor of his father's state, had defrauded him of his rightly inheritance. This delusion dominated Morphy's thinking and behavior, and then relying on his own law training, he filed legal suit against Sybrandt. He was also fearful that Sybrandt would poison him in response to the lawsuit, so Paul retreated to the isolation of the family home and for a while would only eat meals prepared by his mother or his younger unmarried sister Helena, who was still living at home. As was the case for Bobby Fischer's various law suits a century later, Paul's charges were readily dismissed by the New Orleans court.

Morphy's paranoia spread beyond a focus on Sybrandt and he soon began to suspect others of conspiring in some way against him. In one incident he physically attacked a friend, Mr. Binder and further challenged him to a duel of swords. It was this violent incident that led the family and Charles Maurian to consider institutionalization at the Louisiana Retreat house as described earlier (Buck, 1902; Lawson, 2010; Sergeant, 1957).

In the years leading up to his death, Paul's paranoia led him to more seclusion in the family house, and he would interact with only a few family members and trusted friends. His younger sister Helena noting "he was averse to any social intercourse and confined himself to a gloomy retirement apart from his former friends" (Sergeant, 1957, p. 30). Finally, on a hot July day[5] in 1884, after taking a long walk, Morphy sat for a cool bath, which was his daily habit; shortly there-after his mother found him dead in the bathtub. The official cause of death was noted as "congestion of the brain brought on by entering the cold water while very warm after his walk." He was pronounced dead at 2:30 p.m. on July 10. The funeral took place on July 11th at the family home (89 Royal Street) and he was interred in the family tomb at the old St. Louis Cemetery.

Evidence of Paul Morphy's Psychological Illness

The ethical cautions highlighted in Chapters One and Seven with regard to clinically diagnosing Bobby Fischer's mental state, hold as well with regard to my post-mortem assessment of Paul Morphy. Of course, Paul Morphy was never a patient of mine and according to his various biographers (Buck, 1902; Lawson, 2010; Sergeant, 1957), he never received psychological assessment or treatment. My psycholog-ical assessment below is tentative and based on a review of the ar-chival information available on the life of Paul Morphy. Much of the mental health information uncovered by Lawson (2010) is based on letters written by friends, family members, and associates of Mr. Morphy. Thanks to his 30 years of meticulous research, Lawson has uncovered a trove of correspondence regarding Mr. Morphy's per-sonal life, career, and mental state that provided a window into Paul's psychological functioning. In the mid- and late-1800s, writing letters by hand among the upper classes was as popular as e-mail correspon-dence is today, and Lawson has mined virtually everything written on

Morphy in the form of personal letters, diaries, poems, newspaper articles, and chess periodical commentaries and game analyses.

Below I excerpt four letters, all written between 1875 and 1879, that give anecdotal evidence of characteristic symptoms of Paul Morphy's psychological illness. The first two letters were written by Charles Maurian, Paul's life-long best friend who was his classmate at both the Jefferson Academy and Spring Hill College. The two remained close throughout Paul's short life and Paul played chess with Charles even after he had all but abandoned the game.

> I am extremely sorry to say that the report that Mr. Morphy's mind has been somewhat deranged of late, is true. The facts, however, have been greatly exaggerated. He believes that he has many enemies who are attempting to drive him from New Orleans by a system of petty persecutions, etc. This idea has led him to behave on one or two occasions in an extravagant manner, but on all subjects not connected with his particular mania, his mind is apparently as sound as it can be. (From Charles A. Maurian to Captain George H. Mackenzie, dated December. 8, 1875, from Morphy-Voiter, 1926, cited in Lawson, 2010, p. 368)

In the above letter Charles Maurian admitted to Paul Morphy's mental troubles, though he placed the depth of these troubles in some perspective by stating that some of the reports on Paul's illness were exaggerated. By 1875, rumors and reports of Paul's declining mental state were rampant in New Orleans and elsewhere, and some of the reports likely were exaggerated (see a possible example in Lawson, 2010, pp. 310–311). As a loyal friend to Paul and the Morphy family, Maurian attempted to place his friend's symptoms in perspective. Keep in mind that in 1875, the stigma of mental illness was probably quite strong. Even today, with widespread mental health education and national media efforts to destigmatize mental illness, stigma is still a problem that prevents many in need from seeking and receiving psychological treatment. One can imagine the existing stigma in the mid-1800s.

In his letter, Maurian described Paul's mental troubles in terms of delusions of persecution, which on occasion have led Paul to behave in "an extravagant manner," which was a gentle way of saying that Morphy threatened or instigated physical aggression. Finally, as is common in delusional disorders, Maurian stated that on all subjects outside of his delusional ideas Morphy appeared quite normal.

In a letter written two months later to a French newspaper, *La Strategie,* Maurian stated:

> In a letter that I received from you some days ago, you beg me to inform you if it is true that certain rumors about Paul Morphy are true that he may not be right mentally. . . . I am sorry to have to reply to you that these rumors are only too well founded. . . . Mr. Morphy thinks himself the object of the animosity of certain persons who, he claims, are trying to injure him and render life intolerable to him by a regular system of calumnies and petty persecutions. There is no way of persuading him on the point, but on any other subject he is quite reasonable. . . . The fixed idea which possesses him has led him on certain occasions to conduct himself in a somewhat extravagant manner. Thus, about two months ago he strove hard to provoke to a duel a gentleman whom he imagined to be one of his persecutors. (Charles Maurian in a letter to Mr. Preti dated January 18, 1876, translated from *La Strategie,* February, 15, 1876, pp. 33–34, cited in Lawson, 2010, pp. 368–369)

By this point in 1876, Morphy's declining mental state was a topic of discussion throughout the United States and Europe, and Maurian described Morphy's symptoms to his colleague, Mr. Preti, in Paris, France. In the letter, Maurian confirmed the delusional and persecutory nature of Morphy's belief system and specified the nature of his "extravagant" (aggressive) behavior.

The following letter written by a "Mr. D." and published in an 1875 issue of in the *Hartford Times* confirmed symptoms described by Charles Maurian.

> The fact that his mind was not right was observed by his intimate friends some months ago when he was laboring under the delusion that unknown persons were circulating calumnies about him, and imagined that he was the victim of petty persecutions, the aim of which was to drive him from the country. This idea constantly haunted him and drove him at last to the point where he publicly accused several individuals with being concerned in persecuting him. The thing grew upon him until finally he challenged the supposed authors of the imaginary calumnies to mortal combat with deadly weapons.

. . . On all other subjects his mind is apparently sound, and when in company with persons of his liking he converses as rationally as any one. . . . (letter from Mr. D. to Mr. J. E. Orchard, dated December 5, 1875, published in the *Hartford Times,* as cited in Lawson, 2010, pp. 366–367)

A similar set of psychological symptoms was evident in the above letter. First, delusions of persecution, second the intensity of the delusion led Morphy to instigate "combat with deadly weapons" which in this case was a challenge to a duel of swords; and third, when not engaged on the delusional belief topic, he "converses as rationally as any one." Again these are all common symptoms of a delusional disorder defined in Chapter Seven.

The final letter included below was written by a Dr. L. P. Meridith, a chess enthusiast from Cincinnati who was visiting New Orleans and spent time observing Morphy and interviewing his acquaintances:

He professes to be a lawyer of prominence, and, although he has no office, no clients, and spends hours promenading Canal St. daily, he imagines himself so pressed with business that he can not release himself for the briefest time. The great case that absorbs all of his attention is an imaginary one against parties who had charge of an estate left by his father. He demands a detailed, explicit account of everything connected with their administration. . . . At certain hours every day Paul Morphy is as sure to be walking on Canal Street, as Canal Street is sure to be walked on. People shun him for the reason that the least encouragement will result in being compelled to listen for hours to the same old story that everybody knows by heart–that relating to his father's estate. He talks of nothing else, and apparently thinks of nothing else. . . . He is always, while on the street, either moving his lips in soliloquy, removing and replacing his eye-glasses, or smiling and bowing in response to imaginary salutations . . . I have spoken of his imagined salutations, and his pleasant bow and smile, and graceful wave of hand, in response. This must have occurred twenty or thirty times, as he stood behind a massive column for a few minutes, in a position in which it was impossible for any one to see him from the direction in which he looked. (L.P. Meridith letter in Cincinnati Commercial, dated April 16, 1879 cited in Lawson, 2010, pp. 370–371)

This letter addressed additional areas not covered in the first three letters. Though Dr. Meridith highlighted the persecutory delusions noted in the previous letters, he also noted Morphy's obsession with wanting to adjudicate his perceived injustices and is therefore so consumed by these thoughts that he is unable to attend to other matters. The reader will remember from earlier chapters that Bobby Fischer was similarly consumed with lawsuits against journalist Brad Darrach and the World Wide Church of God to the point that it impacted his ability to tend to career and other personal matters. The above letter also highlighted some of Morphy's more obsessive-compulsive habits.

One often-told anecdote that centers on Paul Morphy's obsessive tendencies was first presented by his niece, Regina Morphy-Poitier (1926), in her mini-biography of her uncle. She reported that in his later years he would walk along the verandah (presumably of his family's estate), mumbling in a low voice, "Il plantera la banniere de Castille sur les murs de Madrid au cri de ville gagnee, et le petit Roi s'en ira tout penaud." This phrase translates to "He will plant the banner of Castile upon the walls of Madrid, amidst the cries of the conquered city, and the little king will go away looking very sheepish" (cited in Lawson, 2010, p. 312). The meaning of this statement is unclear, though it has been reported in most of the biographies of Paul Morphy. Psychodynamically speaking, it can represent Paul's internal conflicts with father figures ("the little king"), namely his own father, or perhaps Howard Staunton, the English elder and chess champion, who refused a chess match against Morphy when he traveled to Europe in 1858. However, not much can be made of Morphy's mumblings, and his niece's story had not been validated by any other observer. Regina Morphy-Poitier was a young girl at the time Paul Morphy was said to mutter the often-quoted sentence, and Lawson (2010) questions the accuracy of her memory.

What Happened to Paul Morphy? A Psychological Autopsy

It appears Paul Morphy did suffer from some level of paranoid ideation. Whether the extent and scope of his symptoms were sufficient to merit a formal diagnosis of paranoid personality disorder (as I speculated with Bobby Fischer in Chapter Seven) is difficult to determine with the available archival information. And unlike Bobby Fischer's family history, we know virtually nothing about the mental health/illness history of Morphy's biological relatives. A review of the specific criteria for a diagnosis of paranoid personality disorder outlined in Chapter Seven would indicate that Morphy did in fact meet a number of the criteria, but there is insufficient information, in my opinion, to retrospectively diagnose him as suffering from paranoid personality disorder.

However, a close examination of the archival documentation uncovered by Lawson (2010) does provide strong evidence that Paul Morphy may have developed a delusional disorder. As first presented in Chapter Seven, the diagnostic criteria for Delusional Disorder include (1) nonbizzare delusions for at least one month's duration; (2) ruling out a diagnosis of Schizophrenia; (3) apart from the impact or ramifications of the delusion, functioning is not markedly impaired; (4) absence of long-term mood episodes concurrent to delusional period; and (5) the delusions are not caused by medical or substance use effects (see *Diagnostic and Statistical Manual of Mental Disorders,* 4th ed., [*DSM-IV*], 2000).

From the available evidence it appears that Paul Morphy may have met the criteria for delusional disorder, which is in the class of psychotic disorders (*DSM-IV,* 2000). First, his delusion regarding his brother-in-law and others conspiring against him was certainly nonbizarre (refer back to chapter seven for definitions and examples of bizarre versus nonbizarre delusions); second, he was clearly not schizophrenic (again refer to Chapter Seven for criteria); third, he was able to function and converse well outside the topic of his father's estate (as commented in multiple letters quoted earlier); and fourth, he did not appear to have long-term depressive or mania states (for example he followed his daily routine of walks, baths, and attending the opera and appeared content aside from his delusional belief system). With regard to the fifth criteria for delusional disorder, we cannot be certain to rule out a medical cause for Morphy's delusion. Though he was said to have died of "congestion of the brain," no autopsy was performed so we cannot be sure that Morphy did not have a brain tumor of some sort.

Assuming Morphy did not have an undiscovered brain tumor, it is a good hypothesis that he suffered from delusional disorder. As I hypothesized with regard to Bobby Fischer in Chapter Seven, of the various subtypes of Delusional Disorder, Morphy would fit the Persecutory Type, in which the central theme of the delusion involves the person's belief that he or she is being conspired against, cheated, spied on, followed, poisoned or drugged, maliciously maligned, harassed, or obstructed in the pursuit of long-term goals. Small slights may be exaggerated and become the focus of a delusional system. The focus of the delusion is often on some injustice that must be remedied by legal action (querulous paranoia), and the affected person may engage in repeated attempts to obtain satisfaction by appeal to the courts and other government agencies. Individuals with persecutory delusions are often resentful and angry and may resort to violence against those they believe are hurting them. (American Psychiatric Association, 2000, p. 325)

Paul Morphy certainly believed he was being conspired against, he was obsessed with legal action to fight "the conspirators," and he became very angry and instigated violence on at least two occasions. Thus, acknowledging the limitations of applying modern day psychodiagostic principles to a case study some 135 years old, the leading diagnostic candidate would be a delusional disorder.

Beyond a Clinical Diagnosis

Perhaps more interesting than a clinical diagnosis of Paul Morphy would be an understanding of life circumstances that could help explain his vulnerability to mental illness and the specific manifestation of psychological symptoms. Recalling the *diasthesis stress model* covered in-depth in Chapter Seven, Morphy's mental illness was likely the result of an interaction between biology, or genetic predispositions, and environment and life stress. One hypothetical scenario would be the following.

Paul Morphy was born into a wealthy, successful family in New Orleans, where his father and grandfathers had been very successful and highly respected. There was likely pressure early on to carry the family name well and with distinction. Culturally he had roots in Irish, Spanish, and French Creole traditions and Paul was likely expected to integrate and live up to cultural as well as social class expectations (see Lawson, 2010; Sergeant, 1957). In character and physique, Paul differed from his father, brother and likely male relatives. He was of small and slight stature, with some effeminate features, likely in marked contrast to his paternal lineage where his great grandfather had been a Captain in the Spanish Royal Guard. It is interesting that at Spring Hill College, Paul played the role of Portia in *The Merchant of Venice*. It is not clear if his father knew of this role, or if he did, how he felt about his son playing a female character.

In temperament, Paul was quiet, reflective, meek, kind and gentle. Though we know little of his father's personality, as the Attorney General for Louisiana, it is likely that Judge Alonzo Morphy was a strong, more gregarious and forceful personality than his youngest son Paul. We do know that Alonzo Morphy was strict in terms of his academic expectations for his sons, and he forbade Paul to play chess as a youth except for a few games on Sundays. One can imagine Alonzo Morphy thinking, "My son may be good at chess, but that skill is irrelevant to his necessary academic and career focus."

Lawson (2010) noted that Paul Morphy was baptized (we assume in the Catholic faith), and attended the Jesuit College, Spring Hill. Though Jesuit Universities today are fairly relaxed with regard to expected student comportment and behavior (including at Fordham University where I have taught for the past 26 years), one can imagine that Jesuit higher education in the 1850s would have been more strict and disciplined. Reading Lawson's (2010) biographical masterpiece, one gathers a sense that Paul Morphy's life was fairly controlled by strong parental and societal (upper class European immigrant) forces. With regard to Paul's mother's influence, it is known that she loved her son deeply and catered to him. Aiello (2010, p. ix), in his Editor's Introduction to Lawson's (2010) revised biography, characterized her as "overbearing" and "overprotective." Acknowledging the role of motherhood in mid-nineteenth century European immigrants, Thelcide Morphy's relationship with her son may have been the norm. Nonetheless, the restraining influences of Paul Morphy's parenting, academic, and societal influences may have been a source of stress given his genetic predispositions. Add on to this his sudden fame for chess, an activity not admired or honored as a serious life goal by his father and New Orleans's upper crust society, and we can envision more stress placed on Paul's evolving personality.

Paul Morphy likely had ambivalent feelings about chess. On the one hand, he was amazingly gifted at the game and was the center of attention when playing. His uncle Ernest was particularly proud of his nephew's chess talent and potential. Chess allowed Paul to prove himself in a successful, competitive family and it gave him a sense of identity as the family's and city's best chess player. On the other hand, his mother and father, and New Orleans's upper crust society generally, did not promote chess as a serious pursuit worthy of academic study or a career path. Thus a core part of Morphy's identity was invalidated.

As intimated by both Sergeant (1957) and Lawson (2010), Paul Morphy's time away from family and New Orleans while at Spring Hill College and then during his first European adventure, may have served as a boost to his optimism and sense of well-being–he became free somewhat of the pressures to conform he felt at home. It is known that Paul was happy and productive in his years at Spring Hill College, and save for the frustration of being side-stepped by chess master Howard Staunton, Paul thrived personally and professionally (though he never considered chess a profession, of course) in England and France during his European chess challenges (his father had passed away in 1856 before his U.S. Championship [1856] and European trip [1858]).

Paul Morphy was having such a good time in Europe in 1858–1859, that he had hoped to stay there longer (see details in Lawson, 2010). However, family pressure to return to New Orleans, magnified by the arrival of his older brother-in-law John Sybrandt to oversee and hasten Paul's departure from Europe, was likely a very stressful circumstance for Paul, then only twenty-two years old. Interestingly, as we know, it was John Sybrandt who Paul Morphy would later become obsessed with, paranoid about, and delusional towards.

My sense is that Sybrandt, in coming to "collect" Paul in Europe, was acting as the emissary of the extended Morphy family in New Orleans. In some ways Sybrandt may have taken on the role of family patriarch after Alonzo Morphy's death. It is documented that Sybrandt had some negative impressions of Paul, and he is quoted as telling a friend "P.M. [Paul Morphy] is as lazy as ever, and will not do anything" (Lawson, 2010, p. 289). Keep in mind, that to the Morphy family and New Orleans upper class at this time, playing chess was considered "doing nothing," as it was not considered a serious career pursuit. As intelligent and sensitive as Paul Morphy was, he likely knew of his brother-in-law's mixed impressions of him. Add on to this the fact that Sybrandt (and not Paul [an attorney] or Edward Morphy) was declared by Alonzo Morphy the executor of his estate, may not have sat well with Paul.

This sequence of events and negative associations with Sybrandt may have directed Paul's delusion of persecution to focus on his brother-in-law (as discussed in detail earlier in this chapter). In earlier chapters I discussed why " the Jews" may have become the focus of Bobby Fischer's delusion and paranoia. Of course, determining the exact links and reasons why a particular topic or person or group of persons becomes the outlet for one's paranoia or delusional thinking is a challenging and sometimes impossible task; thus I remind my readers that my views here are working hypotheses only, and not fact.

After returning from three sojourns in Europe (see Appendix D for specific dates of each trip), not succeeding in his law career, not playing chess (except for an occasional game with a close friend) for creative cognitive stimulation, Paul had more time to contemplate perceived offenses against him. This free time, layered on top of possible genetic predispositions to paranoid thinking (as we discussed with Bobby Fischer in Chapter Seven) may have put him at increased risk for psychopathology. Psychoanalyst and chess Grandmaster Reuben Fine hypothesized that chess playing delayed the escalation and manifestation of Morphy's mental illness. This hypothesis was also attributed to Bobby Fischer's psychological profile.

Another major stressor impacting Paul Morphy's psyche was career frustration. He was brilliant on the rule of Louisiana law, and not to be taken seriously as a lawyer in New Orleans was likely a severe blow to his self-esteem and sense of identity, and likely weighed on his reservoir of coping skills. And, as was the case with Bobby Fischer, Paul never received mental health treatment that could have helped him understand and cope with his developing mental illness. Naturally, the Irish/Spanish/French Creole attitudes toward mental illness and its treatment (for a treatise on culture and mental health see the *Handbook of Multicultural Counseling* [Ponterotto, Casas, Suzuki, & Alexander, 2010]) , and the limited status (relative to today) of professional counseling and treatment, contributed to Morphy being cared for by only his mother and sister in his final years. Clearly, Morphy may have benefitted from psychotherapy at this critical period in his life.

Thus, as in Bobby Fischer's case, growing isolation in concert with genetic predispositions and environmental stressors led to Morphy's increasing symptoms of paranoia, obsessive traits, and a delusional disorder. Paul Morphy died in relative isolation, but with the loving and devoted care of his mother and sister, as well as support from life-long friend Charles Maurian.

A Note on Paul Morphy's Sexuality

Interestingly, one topic that has been virtually ignored in all the biographies (Buck, 1902; Edge, 1859; Lawson, 2010; Sergeant, 1957) and biographical sketches (Kurtz, 1993) of Paul Morphy concerns his romantic interests and sexual orientation. Lawson documented the many female friends of Morphy's, including nobility—princesses, count-esses, duchesses—who wanted to be around him and play chess with him. We know Paul was pleased by the company of these and other women, but we do not know if Paul had intimate, sexual feelings towards women. In one letter published in the *New York Evening Post* (May 31, 1859; Paul was in New York on his way back to New Orleans from Europe) and quoted by Lawson (2010, p. 219) it is noted that a "mysterious" female chess player called upon Morphy unexpectedly to challenge him to chess. According to the story, after the game of two hours was drawn [I imagine Morphy purposely drew the game as a chivalrous gesture] and the lady had left, Paul and his friends set out to try to determine who the woman was, but to no avail. The accuracy of this story cannot be documented, and regardless, Paul's possible interest in a female visitor is not proof of his heterosexuality.

Lawson (2010, p. 219) did venture to conclude that "While little is known of the women in Morphy's life, he seems to have had some attraction for them." However, there is no evidence in the hundreds of documents uncovered and analyzed by Lawson (2010) that Paul ever had a girlfriend or sexual relationships with women. Likewise there is no evidence of homosexuality in the historical records on Paul Morphy's personal life. It is interesting that Paul Morphy's two closest emotional bonds and connections (outside of his mother and younger sister) were two men: Frederick Edge, who accompanied him as his secretary on his first European chess challenges; and lifelong friend Charles Maurian. There is no evidence that Morphy was sexually attracted to either man. In summary, Morphy's sexuality, in all respects, remains a mystery to historians and biographers who study his life.

From a psychological perspective, to fully understand a human being we must endeavor to explore the person's multiple and intersecting identities, which include racial identity, religious identity, social class, ethnic identity, immigration and migration history, career identity, gender identity, and sexual orientation identity (Ponterotto, Utsey, & Pedersen, 2006). This topic with respect to Paul Morphy deserves further study and would make for a good master's thesis or doctoral dissertation. It is likely that respect for privacy and the stigma of discussing sex and sexual orientation among the upper classes of New Orleans in the mid-1880s may be in part responsible for the lack of letters or diaries that broach these topics regarding Morphy. Also, to my knowledge, Paul Morphy never kept journals or diaries, so it is difficult to know the inner workings of his mind and feelings.

Similarities and Differences in the Lives and Mental Illness of Morphy and Fischer

Without question, Paul Morphy and Bobby Fischer were the United States' two most celebrated chess champions. They were the only North American chess players to achieve the title of World Chess Champion, officially in Fischer's case, and unofficially in Morphy's case. These two enigmatic and iconic personalities captured the imagination and hopes of millions of chess players worldwide. Sadly, both men lapsed into ill psychological health. Fischer's psychological problems were detected earlier in his life, whereas Morphy's psychological decline was documented only after his sudden retirement from competitive chess. It is likely however, that symptoms of mental illness in Paul Morphy appeared before friends and family began writing about them in letters in 1875.

In my opinion, the mental illness progression of both champions was somewhat similar, with both having some obsessive/compulsive tendencies, both becoming paranoid, and both developing delusions of persecution. In the end, they both died at relatively young ages, in relative isolation and seclusion, open to trusting but a handful of family and friends. Table 8.1 below, summarizes some of the similarities in the lives of Bobby Fischer and Paul Morphy.

Table 8.1

SIMILARITIES IN THE LIVES OF BOBBY FISCHER AND PAUL MORPHY

1. Intelligent with natural gift for spatial relationships, memory, intense focusing ability, and planning forward (logical and sequenced analysis).
2. Child prodigies who learned the game of chess around 6 years of age and became exceptionally good a few years later.
3. Both played spectacular Queen Sacrifice games (while playing the Black pieces) that were momentous games in their respective centuries, Morphy defeating Louis Paulsen in 1857 and Fischer beating Donald Byrne in 1956. (It is very likely, given Fischer's knowledge of the chess literature by age 13, that he had studied Morphy's Queen Sacrifice game a century earlier.)
4. Facility for learning languages.
5. Both found unfit for military duty. Fischer failed draft board physical during Vietnam War; Morphy was discouraged from military service on or off (diplomatic service) the battlefield by General Beauregard during Civil War.
6. The only North American players reaching the status of World Chess Champion; Morphy (unofficially) in 1858, and Fischer (officially) in 1972.
7. Returned to the United States after World Champion victories abroad to public celebrations and acknowledgements, and a hero-like welcome.
8. After World Championship victories withdrew to various degrees from competitive chess play.
9. Never defended their world titles in official matches or tournaments.
10. Though they both stopped playing competitive chess in their prime, both kept up with chess events and tournament results.
11. As they withdrew from the public chess arena, national interest in the game of chess subsided.
12. Began to demonstrate paranoid symptoms.
13. Developed delusional systems.
14. Died at relatively young ages (Morphy at 47 years; Fischer at 64 years) in relative isolation, trusting only a handful of people.

Though there are noted similarities in the lives of Bobby Fischer and Paul Morphy, particularly with regard to their respective levels of chess genius and mental illness, there are many more differences among the two men. For one, playing a century apart, Morphy was raised Catholic in an intact, prominent, well-to-do family in the South. Fischer, of Jewish parentage, and living most of his childhood in New York, was raised by a single parent who was always struggling financially and was subjected to ongoing surveillance by the FBI (refer back to Chapter Four). Morphy had a stable home in New Orleans and attended two of the best schools in the South, while Fischer lived in multiple cities and attended various schools before the age of ten years. Though both were highly intelligent, Fischer's intellectual energy was directed almost exclusively to chess (until 1972), while Morphy was a renaissance scholar, in the truest sense of the word, from childhood.

Naturally for Fischer, chess was life ("All I ever want to do is play chess"; "I give 98% of my mental energy to chess," Brady, 1973, pp. 17, 74); for Morphy chess was socialized in him to be but a diversion from real life pursuits ("I am more strongly confirmed than ever in the belief that the time devoted to chess is literally frittered away," Lawson, 2010, p. 288). Fischer played competitive chess for over 20 years (from the early 1950s through 1972, and reemerging in 1992 for one match), while Morphy played high level competitive chess for only a few years (particularly 1857–1859).

As a young adult Bobby Fischer was a tall, athletic, masculine presence; Morphy was small and slight, with child-size hands[6] and a boyish appearance. Fischer had romantic involvements and was sexually active with some women; Paul's sexuality appears to be a mystery to researchers, and he had no sexual partners to anyone's knowledge. Table 8.2 on the next two pages, summarizes some of the major differences in the lives of Fischer and Morphy.

During the lives of Paul Morphy and Bobby Fischer there was tremendous pride and hope among the millions of chess fans in the United States and worldwide. Both men were brilliant visionaries at the chessboard and their distinct and unique personalities captured worldwide attention. As these world champions of the royal game abandoned competitive play, secluded themselves in relative isolation, and became mentally ill, the pride and hope of chess players turned to sorrow and despair. The life stories of Fischer and Morphy are both fascinating and sad. In the end, these men died virtually alone with no offspring to speak their legacy. Yet their influence and impact on the game of chess was so significant that their games will likely live on, worldwide, for as long as humans walk this earth. Despite their challenges and psychological struggles, let us honor their memory and legacy.

Table 8.2
DIFFERENCES IN THE LIVES OF BOBBY FISCHER AND PAUL MORPHY

Bobby Fischer	*Paul Morphy*
Product of single-parent, poor family.	Product of an intact family of means and status.
Lived in various apartments and cities during early childhood.	Lived in same beautiful house during childhood.
Singular career focus on chess for most of early life, at least from around 1949 through 1972.	Chess was never seen as legitimate career; had many other interests, and was an attorney at law.
Voracious reader of chess materials; by the age of thirteen had read and absorbed an international body of chess literature.	By the age of thirteen had not read any chess books.
Low levels of formal education, not a strong student, dropped out of high school at the age of 16.	Gifted academically in many topical areas, highly and broadly educated, received a law degree at age 20.
Allowed by mother to play chess extensively as child and adolescent.	Limited by parents to playing only three or four games of chess on Sundays.
Played against very good players starting in childhood and adolescence.	Quite isolated from very good players during youth.
Tall, athletic who played various sports with proficiency.	Small, slight (5 feet 4 inches), with aversion to sports and athletics (though learned fencing at father's insistence).
Insisted that chess be respected as a valued intellectual profession and duly rewarded financially and in terms of status.	Thought of chess only as a game, a diversion, not to be taken at all seriously as a career.
Considered to have a "difficult" personality, at times very challenging to be around.	Considered the epitomy of a "southern gentlemen," always respectful, kind, engaging, a pleasure to be around.
Clearly heterosexual and interested in and sexually active with women.	Unclear as to Morphy's sexual orientation, and does not seem to have had any romantic/sexual partners.

Chapter Nine

ON THE RELATIONSHIP BETWEEN GENIUS AND MADNESS–ARE CHESS MASTERS MORE VULNERABLE TO MENTAL ILLNESS?

I object to being called a chess genius, because I consider myself an all-around genius who just happens to play chess.
(Bobby Fischer as cited in Chun, 2002, p. 87)

At the same time Fischer had some abnormalities. For example, he hated communists and was a terrible anti-Semite, although his mother was a practicing Jew. Yes, at certain moments he could be unpleasant and even insufferable. But he was a genius, which means he had the right to certain oddities, as after all genius is an abnormality in itself.
(Mark Taimanov, 2011)

I n the chess literature there are numerous stories of elite chess players "gone mad." In the United States, the stories of the North Americans Paul Morphy and Bobby Fischer are the most common. But the hypothesized association between chess genius and the development of mental illness extends back in time to at least the early nineteenth century. A number of prominent chess authors have speculated on the relationship between elite chess talent and mental illness. For example Paul Hoffman (2007), in his popular book, *King's Gambit,* stated the following: "I believe that madness is rampant in championship chess, particularly in the tier of players just below the top. After all, to reach the pinnacle of chess requires a certain psychological stability" (p. 17).

Chess master and renowned chess teacher, Bruce Pandolfini, stated the following:

Let's face it . . . there are more unbalanced people in chess than in your average profession or activity, although perhaps no more than in other arts. But that's because the chess community is wonderfully accepting–everyone is welcome to play and you don't need any social skills to succeed. . . . People whose sense of self derives from how they do at chess, because they have so little else going on in their lives, are the ones who are likely to crack up from the pressure of tournament play. . . . Fischer was a case in point. (cited in Hoffman, 2007, pp. 75–76)

Noted chess author David Shenk who wrote *The Immortal Game: A History of Chess* (Shenk, 2006), in commenting on Bobby Fischer's steady psychological decline after his 1972 World Championship victory, noted that:

It is impossible, of course, to definitively diagnose Fischer or any other individual based on sketchy glimpses of public behavior. But it is equally impossible to ignore or deny the pattern: a significant number of the world's most accomplished chess masters have succumbed over time to delusional paranoia, violent feelings of persecution, and severe detachment from the real world–a combination that psychologists recognize as falling into the category of schizophrenia. (p. 145)

As I highlighted in my psychological autopsies of Bobby Fischer (Chapter Seven) and Paul Morphy (Chapter Eight), I do not believe either suffered from schizophrenia, but the overarching point raised by both Shenk (2006) and Hoffman (2007) is that there may be an association between chess genius and mental illness. In this chapter I examine this hypothesized relationship more systematically through a review of relevant research literature.

In the first section of this chapter I revisit some anecdotes describing the purported sad mental health fate of a number of elite chess players over the past three centuries. It is important to emphasize that the chess masters reviewed in this section were only alleged to have some degree of mental illness. I have not conducted (or uncovered previous) psychological autopsies on these individuals.

After brief comments on some 15 elite chess players who may have suffered from mental illness, the second section of the chapter examines, from a more empirical standpoint, the relationship between creativity/original thinking (a hallmark of chess mastery) and vulnerability to mental illness. More specifically, does research support a relationship between creativity and mental illness?

MENTAL ILLNESS AMONG CHESS LEGENDS OF THE PAST

Austrian-born Wilhelm Steinitz (1836–1900), considered the first official world chess champion, told a friend "I have for years, been the victim of a nervous affection which often entails loss of memory and utterly incapacitated me for mental work" (Shenk, 2006, pp. 142–143). Over time Steinitz became more mentally ill, perhaps psychotic, and was for a time confined to a Moscow asylum. One story goes that he insisted that he had played chess with God over an invisible telephone wire–his memory was that he won that game (Fine, 2009; Shenk, 2006).

At the turn of the nineteenth century, Polish chess sensation Akiba Rubinstein (1882–1961) was clearly one of the strongest players in the world. Though he never had the chance to challenge then champion Emanuel Lasker for the world title, many at the time thought him to be the equal, if not the superior, to Lasker. Reportedly, Rubinstein suffered throughout his life from pathological shyness, and eventually suffered from severe paranoia to the point of needing long-term psychiatric hospitalization (Shenk, 2006).

The fourth official world chess champion, Russian-born Alexander Alekhine (1892–1946), apparently succumbed to alcoholism and was hospitalized in a psychiatric facility. Alekhine is also infamous as a Nazi collaborator (Fine, 2009; Shenk, 2006).

Carlos Torre-Repetto (1905–1978), Mexico's first Grandmaster, became a household name in the chess world when in 1925 he defeated then World Champion Emanuel Lasker at the Moscow international tournament. However, Torre-Repetto only played elite competitive chess for two years (reminiscent of the North American Paul Morphy) before being hospitalized for mental illness. One scene depicts him taking off all of his clothes on a New York City bus (Pierogy, 2010; Shenk, 2006).

Tony Miles (1955–2001) was the 1974 World Junior Chess Champion and the first chess player in England to achieve the exalted status of Grandmaster. Reportedly Miles began to experience episodes of paranoia, believing that a fellow British grandmaster was out to harm him. Like Torre-Repetto discussed earlier, Miles would suddenly take off his clothes, in his case he undressed in a tournament hall and on a city bus. At one point he was arrested outside Margaret Thatcher's residence on 10 Downing Street and subsequently was hospitalized for two months (Hoffman, 2007; O'Fee, 2008). Tony Miles died at the age of 46 from untreated diabetes.

The North American chess master Raymond Weinstein finished 3rd in the 1960–1961 U.S. Chess Championship behind Bobby Fischer and William Lombardy. Apparently, Weinstein developed schizophreia and was permanently institutionalized on Ward's Island in New York City (Shenk, 2006).

Over the years a number of elite chess players have committed suicide by jumping off of bridges or out of high windows. Among the first to end his or her life in this way was German chess master Curt von Bardeleben in the year 1924. According to Hoffman (2007), it is likely that Von Bardeleben's suicide was the stimulus for the character Alexander Ivanovich Luzhin in Nabokov's (1964) book, the *Luzhin Defense,* which was also made into a major motion picture titled *The Luzhin Defence,* starring John Turturro as the troubled chess genius.

Other documented suicides by jumping included Armenian international master Karen Grigorian and Russian international master Gregory Ilivitzky, both in 1989. Roughly a decade later, the Latvian international master Alvis Vitolins jumped to his death in 1997, and Lembert Oll, the Estonian grandmaster, committed suicide in 1999. More recently, in 2006, Oxford University-bound English talent, Jessie Gilbert, jumped to her death from her eighth-floor hotel window while participating in a tournament in Pardubire, Czech Republic. This slate of jumping suicides, all reported in Hoffman (2007), transcended nationality and gender.

Shenk (2006) listed additional elite chess players over the centuries who succumbed to mental illness. His list included: World class player Gustav Neumann, who left competition in 1872 due to mental illness; German player Johannes Minckwitz, who committed suicide by throwing himself in front of an oncoming train in 1901; and Polish player George Rotlewi, who in 1911 at the age of 22 years was forced out of chess competition due to mental illness. Shenk (2006) also highlighted that the great Latvian chess player and theoretician, Aron Nimzowitsch, also likely had some degree of mental illness as reflected in paranoid and bizarre behavior.

What is to be made of the association between chess genius and mental illness? Are brain mechanisms of highly creative and original thinkers different than those in your average person? If so, could those brain differences be linked in some way with susceptibility to mental illness? To answer these questions, it is important to examine a bit of the research on the association between creativity and mental illness.

A Neurological Link Between Creativity and Mental Illness

History is replete with stories of creative and original thinkers who succumbed to mental illness. Luminaries who come immediately to mind include the painter, Vincent van Gogh, the authors Sylvia Plath and Ernest Hemingway, the mathematician John Forbes Nash, Jr. (played by Russell Crowe in the movie *A Beautiful Mind*), and of course, the great North American-born chess champions Paul Morphy and Bobby Fischer.

In a carefully controlled empirical study, Andreasen (1987) compared prevalence rates of mental illness in 30 creative writers against a matched control group. Results of the study indicated a substantially higher rate of mental illness, particularly affective disorder (no subjects from either group suffered from psychosis) in the creative writers. Furthermore, there was also a higher prevalence of mental illness and creativity in the writers' first-degree relatives, suggesting genetic mediation of traits. A question to consider at this point is whether there is any possible link between creativity and mental illness.

Research over the last decade has uncovered some association between high levels of creativity and mental illness. Neural processes implicated in this association include genes and neurotransmitters. For example, a variant of the gene Neuregulin 1, which is important to developing and strengthening communication between neurons, has been associated with a higher risk of developing serious mental disorders such as bipolar disorder and schizophrenia (Keri, Kiss, & Kelemen, 2009; Keri, Kiss, Seres, & Kelemen, 2008).

In one study conducted by a researcher at Semmelweil University in Hungary (Keri, 2009), healthy volunteer participants who had the particular genetic variant of Neuregulin 1 (that had been previously implicated in mental illness) were more likely than those without the genetic variant to score higher on tests of creativity and had accumulated a greater number of tangible achievements over their lifetimes. Keri's (2009) sample consisted of highly intelligent (mean IQ = 124) healthy volunteers, and this researcher surmises that the Neuregulin 1 variant may reduce cognitive inhibition (thus allowing in more stimuli to the brain), thus facilitating creativity. At present, it is unknown whether Keri's results would generalize to individuals with average or lower IQ.

In a second study, researchers representing the Karolinska Institute in Stockholm and the National Institutes of Health (NIH) in the United States, have shown that the dopamine (a brain neurotransmitter) system in highly creative healthy individuals in some ways resembles that seen in individuals suffering with schizophrenia (de Manzano et al., 2010). These authors highlighted that creativity had been previously linked to a slightly higher risk of schizophrenia and bipolar disorder, and that high levels of creativity have been shown to be somewhat more common in individuals who have a history of mental illness within the biological family.

De Manzano et al.'s (2010) research examined the Dopamine D2 receptors and their results indicated that the dopamine system of highly creative healthy individuals was similar to that found in persons suffering with schizophrenia. The similar trait implicated may revolve around divergent thinking and the ability to make unusual or bizarre associations. More specifically, de Manzano et al. (2010) found that highly creative healthy individuals who did well on tests of divergent thinking and problem solving exhibited lower density of D2 receptors in the thalamus than did the less creative individuals. Individuals with schizophrenia are also prone to exhibit lower D2 density in the thalamus.

De Manzano's (2010) research team hypothesized that fewer D2 receptors in the thalamus indicate a lower degree of signal filtering and thus a higher flow of information relayed from the thalamus to other parts of the brain. Signal filtering is the organism's unconscious capacity to ignore stimuli (e.g., information, sounds, lights) that evolutionary experience has shown as irrelevant or nonessential to its survival needs. Thus individuals with lower density D2 receptors in the thalamus have more information and stimuli entering their consciousness—this could lead to creative, original "outside the box" thinking in healthy individuals, or it could lead to stimulus overload and bizarre thinking in individuals with mental illness.

A third and earlier study from a joint team of researchers from Harvard University (the United States) and the University of Toronto (Canada) (Carson, Peterson, & Higgins, 2003) appears to support the findings of de Manzano et al.'s (2010) research team. It appears that brains of highly creative people have lower levels of latent inhibition and are thus more open to incoming stimuli from the surrounding environment. In this manner, latent inhibition works like signal filtering (discussed previously in the deManzano et al., 2010 study) as an evolutionary adaptation to selectively screen out external stimuli not necessary to the organism's survival and advancement.

The Carson et al. (2003) research team sampled Harvard undergraduate students and found that eminent creative achievers in their sample were seven times more likely to have low latent inhibition scores. The researchers reasoned that creative individuals remain in contact with information constantly streaming in from the environment. Such sensitivity to environmental stimuli may contribute to original thinking when combined with higher IQ, good working memory, and other cognitive skills. For example, consider a given chess position that may lead to possibly 20 different next moves, but only one or two moves may be really strong options. A chess master needs to absorb and analyze the stimuli (the current chess position and possible next move) and use other cognitive decision skills to select and make the strongest possible move. Carson et al. (2003) believed that low levels of latent inhibition and exceptional flexibility in thinking might predispose some individuals to great creative accomplishments and others to mental illness.

Are Elite Chess Players More Prone to Mental Illness?

As reviewed in the previous section, recent research has uncovered some link between brain mechanisms of highly creative people and those of individuals with serious mental illness. However, neurobiological research on this topic is still in its infancy and research studies have necessarily (for ethical reasons) relied on correlational designs that cannot imply causation. It cannot be said that creativity leads to mental illness or that mental illness leads to high levels of creativity. All we know is that some gene variants and some neurotransmitter action is similar in the brains of highly creative people and individuals with serious mental illness. For certain, most highly creative people are not mentally ill, and most mentally ill individuals are not particularly creative.

Serious mental illness transcends culture, socioeconomic status, creativity and intelligence levels, and vocations. Are creative, original thinkers generally, and elite chess players specifically, more likely to develop mental illness? Earlier in this chapter brief profiles of elite chess players who purportedly suffered from mental illness were highlighted. Though a good number of players were highlighted there are actually millions of individuals who play chess worldwide. Thus, logic would indicate that only a very small percentage of chess players suffer from mental illness. It would be instructive to examine the incidence of mental illness in the population at large, and in specific vocations to gather a more specific sense of the prevalence of mental illness.

Generally speaking, rates of mental illness parallel those of physical illness. More specifically, a national epidemiological survey of roughly 35,000 U.S. adults found that the "incidence rates of substance, mood and anxiety disorders were comparable to or greater than the rates of lung cancer, stroke and cardiovascular disease" (Grant et al., 2009, p. 1051). Over the last two decades there have been numerous national studies assessing the incidence rates of mental disorders. A number of these studies distinguish between "serious mental illness" and "any mental illness." Both categories of illness involve mental, behavioral, or emotional disorders that meet the criteria for diagnosis according to the *Diagnostic and Statistical Manual of Mental Disorders* (*DSM-IV-TR*, American Psychiatric Association, 2000). However, those individuals categorized as having a "serious mental illness" experience functional impairment which limits one or more major life activities. The category of "any mental illness" can include individuals of varying levels of functioning and impairment.[1]

Across many national studies over the past two decades, the findings on the incidence rates of mental illness are fairly consistent. In any given year, roughly 5–6 percent of North Americans suffer from "serious mental illness," whereas anywhere from 18 percent to 28 percent (median rate of 22% across numerous national surveys) of the population suffers from "any mental illness" (The WHO World Mental Health Survey Consortium, 2004; U.S. Department of Health and

Human Services, 2009).[2] Given both Bobby Fischer (see Chapter Seven) and Paul Morphy (see Chapter Eight) likely suffered from "serious mental illness" because they experienced "serious functional impairment" in at least one major life activity (i.e., career development), each would be part of the 5–6 percent incidence rate figure noted above.

Are Certain Career Paths More Hazardous to One's Mental Health?

To my knowledge, there has been no national or international study specifically comparing mental illness incidence rates of professional chess players to individuals in other professions or in the general population. However, some research has examined mental illness incidence rates across broad categories of job titles, for example, executive/managerial, professional specialty, semi-skilled manual, farming, and so forth. For example, a national Canadian study found that roughly 8 percent of employed workers (ages 15–54) suffered from mental illness. Of this 8 percent, the largest number of persons suffering from anxiety, affective, or substance use disorders was in "unskilled manual jobs" with 7.2 percent of such workers suffering from one of the aforementioned mental illnesses. Other job categories with relatively higher incidence rates of mental illness were "high-level management" (6.4% of such workers suffered from mental illness), and "skilled clerical" (at 6.2%). The Canadian job categories with the smallest percentage of mentally ill workers were "technician" (2.5%), "semi-skilled manual" (3.2%), and "supervisor" (3.3%). The job category that would include professional chess players in the Canadian labor statistics is the category of "professional." Mental illness rates (again, just looking at anxiety, depression, and substance use disorders) in the "professional" category fell at 4.4 percent (Dewa, Lesage, Goering, & Caveen, 2004; Dewa & Lin, 2000).

In a large-scale U.S. study (Mechanic, Bilder, & McAlpine, 2002) of close to 90,000 employed adults (ages 18–65), roughly 2.2 percent reported "any mental illness" and .44 percent reported "serious mental illness" (including schizophrenia, paranoid states, mood disorders, and other nonorganic psychoses). Of those classified with "serious mental illness" and "any mental illness," 18.2 percent and 14.4 percent, respectively, worked in the occupational category of "service, except protective and household," and 14.8 percent and 17.2 percent, respectively, worked in "administrative support, including clerical." The occupation categories with the lowest relative representation of "serious mental illness" and "any mental illness" were "farming, forestry, and fishing" (1.3% and 1.4% respectively), and "protective service" (1.7% and 1.6% respectively). The occupational category that would per-force include professional chess players is termed "professional specialty" and of those with "serious" or "any" mental illness in the sample, 11.9 percent and 15.9 percent, respectively, were included in this occupational grouping.

Well, What are We to Make of this Data?

To summarize some of the main research findings reviewed in this chapter, it is important to note that mental illness is fairly widespread and transcends age, gender, and occupations. Roughly speaking, 22 percent of North Americans could be said to suffer from some form of mental illness, while roughly 5 percent can be said to suffer from serious mental illness. There are some differential mental illness incidence rates based on broad occupational categories, but at present, no national or international study of mental illness rates specifically in elite chess players or chess professionals has been published to this author's knowledge. As such, at the present time, we cannot state that mental illness is greater in chess players than in other professions.

Though there are many stories of select chess masters who display strong signs of mental illness (as with the 15 chess masters reviewed at the beginning of this chapter), the research base at this point does not support any definitive link between elite chess skill and mental illness. There may be some neurological links between processes involved in exceptional creativity (absorbing and processing extensive stimuli) and in psychosis, yet this research is still in its infancy. Exceptional creativity is a hallmark of success in many fields—chess, art, music, finance, dance choreography, science—and thus chess cannot be singled out for association with mental illness. It is also important to remember our discussion of the diathesis stress model (Zuckerman, 1999), which considers a biosocial explanation of psychopathology where genetic predispositions interact with environmental triggers to set off mental illness.

An important area for psychological research on exceptional creativity and "giftedness" is to longitudinally map the paths of gifted youth both to healthy expression of creativity and the development of mental illness. Given a group of gifted children, what early childhood and environmental factors determine which will develop their gifts in healthy and balanced ways, and which will succumb to stress and start to develop serious symptoms of mental illness? The answer to this question is multifaceted and likely involves the complex interaction of different levels of genetic predispositions (for thinking patterns and behavior) and early family, school, and community environmental influences.

In all probability, given national incidence rates of mental illness, we can expect 22 percent of chess players to suffer from some level of mental illness, and 5 percent to suffer from serious mental illness. Thus for example, if we consider the U.S. Chess Federation and its membership of some 80,000 players, it is reasonable to estimate 22 percent or 17,600 would be coping with some form of mental illness, and 5 percent or 4,000 might be suffering from serious mental illness in a given year. If we look at the pool of chess grandmasters, the category befitting Bobby Fischer and Paul Morphy, a recent Wikipedia.com entry estimates over 1,300 grandmasters. Thus 22 percent or 286 grandmasters may be coping with some level of mental illness, and 5 percent or 65 could be classified as having a serious mental illness. It is likely that Bobby Fischer and Paul Morphy (refer back to Chapters Seven and Eight) would have fallen in this latter category in a given year in their lives.

Perhaps more important to our discussion of incidence rates across professions is the well documented finding that roughly half of all individuals suffering from mental illness nationally and worldwide do not receive necessary treatment (The WHO World Mental Health Survey Consortium, 2004; U.S. Department of Health and Human Services, 2009). Patterns of later life mental illness are associated with childhood or adolescent onset (Kessler & Wang, 2008) and therefore, early assessment and intervention must be a priority for educational and mental health professionals as well as political and public policy leaders. It is interesting to speculate how Bobby Fischer's life and career would have turned out had he received early and consistent mental health treatment, and it is this topic that forms the focus of the next chapter.

Chapter Ten

IF ONLY? PSYCHOLOGICAL TREATMENT OF BOBBY FISCHER AND FAMILY

I don't believe in psychology, I believe in good moves.
(Bobby Fischer as cited in Brady, 1973, p. 230)

If Fischer becomes more aware of his psychological conflicts it should improve his game.
(Fine, 2008, p. 91)

This chapter explores the "what if" question regarding psychological treatment of Bobby Fischer. Would Bobby Fischer have benefitted from counseling and psychotherapy at various points in his life? Could psychological treatment have derailed him from his singular pursuit of supreme chess mastery and the World Chess Championship title? Or could Bobby have led a happier and more balanced life with psychological treatment? Naturally, we will never know the answer to these questions, and, I remind my readers that Bobby Fischer was never officially diagnosed with a mental disorder. However, it is clear that Bobby exhibited troubled behavior and thinking patterns at various points in life, and thus the question about the impact of possible psychological treatment is a worthy one.

This final chapter of the *A Psychobiography of Bobby Fischer: Understanding the Genius, Mystery, and Psychological Decline of a World Chess Champion* begins with a look back to the final chapter in Bobby Fischer's life.

BOBBY FISCHER'S FINAL HOURS

In the last chapter of his life, Bobby Fischer returned to the land of his historic, earth-shattering victory over Boris Spassky over three decades earlier–Reykjavik, Iceland. Thanks to a group of loyal Icelandic supporters, who remembered well the summer of 1972 in Reykjavik, and who are sometimes referred to as the "committee of seven," Fischer secured full Icelandic citizenship in 2005. However, over time, Fischer alienated many of this "committee of seven" due to his irrational, circular-thinking-anchored, and unrelenting anti-Semitic and anti-American monologues (Carlin, 2011). Throughout his adolescence and adult life, Fischer would alienate former friends, colleagues, and even family members, and his final years in Reykjavik (2005–2008) were no different.

Two of the "committee of seven" who remained extremely loyal to Fischer throughout his last months alive were Reykjavik neighbor, Gardar Sverrisson, and his friend Magnus Skulason, who also happened to be a revered psychiatrist in Iceland. Dr. Skulason was with Fischer in his final days of life, and as an experienced psychiatrist his insights on Bobby Fischer are very insightful. In an interview Dr. Skulason gave to journalist John Carlin (2011) of *The Guardian/The Observer,* he observed that there was a big gap between Bobby Fischer's intellectual ability and his emotional maturity. Skulason commented that Bobby "looked at life the way a little boy does, and like a child he always wanted to have his own way and got angry if you refused him" (Carlin, 2011, p. 6). Dr. Skulason went on further to hypothesize that:

> It was an extreme burden for a young boy who grew up from the age of two with a single mother who was very often outside the home . . . he was lonely as a child, I believe, and also poor. Chess was a refuge. He built up his own walls, an immature, aggressive sort of protection in which trust–a basic necessity of healthy social interaction–was practically banished. (Carlin, 2011, p. 6)

Dr. Skulason was at Fischer's bedside the night leading up to his death. He shared with journalist Carlin (2011) this poignant final scene:

I would speak in a monologue and he would fall asleep, like a baby. Then he would wake up with aches and pains and I would press some grapes and give him a glass of juice, or some goat's milk, which unfortunately he could not hold down. Once, towards dawn, he woke up and said his feet ached and asked if I could massage them. I tried my best, and it was then that he said his last words to me and, as far as I know, to anybody. Responding to my hands on his feet he said, with a terrible gentleness, 'Nothing is as healing as the human touch. (pp. 6–7)

Bobby Fischer was isolated and alienated from others much of his life. Given that his lack of trust developed early on and resulted from an interaction of hereditary predispositions for suspiciousness, and a frenetic, hectic, and unstable early home and academic environment (refer back to Chapters Six and Seven), Bobby perhaps never established a basic sense of trust which is a critical psychosocial development step outlined by pioneering psychologist Erik Erikson (1950). Bobby may have craved trust and emotional intimacy, and thus his final words to friend Magnus Skulason are poignant indeed. Could counseling and early intervention in Bobby's life have helped him learn to trust himself and others? Let us now turn to possible psychological interventions that I strongly believe could have helped Bobby Fischer and his family.

Psychological Counseling and the Fischer Family

Over the one-half century since Regina Fischer first brought Bobby to the Children's Psychiatric Division of Brooklyn Jewish Hospital, the fields of psychology and psychiatry have advanced considerably. Furthermore, the stigma associated with receiving mental health treatment among immigrant families in the 1940s and 1950s has attenuated considerably in the present decade, and the availability of a wide variety of mental health services, and state-of-the-art psychotropic medications is abundantly available. If Bobby were born in the present decade, psychological treatment for him, and supportive services for his mother and sister, may have included the following interventions. I begin with a focus on his mother and sister, and then move to possible interventions for Bobby himself.

Psychological Support for Regina and Joan Fischer

First, Regina Fischer's psychosocial stress as a subject of FBI sur-veillance would have been reduced with appropriate interdisciplinary treatment. As a single mother of two young children with limited fi-nancial means, she could have received financial assistance and legal advocacy with regard to dealing with the FBI surveillance and marked intrusion into her and her family's lives. She might have received sup-portive counseling to validate her feelings of being overwhelmed as well as cognitive-behavioral counseling to help her develop coping strategies for dealing with her suspiciousness and financial troubles. Given Bobby's difficult temperament from early childhood, Regina could have benefitted from parent training and/or be guided to relat-ed parenting support and financial resources.

With the lion's share of attention in previous biographies and re-ports related to the Fischer family being directed toward Bobby and Regina Fischer, it is important to incorporate Bobby's sister Joan into any comprehensive discussion of the Fischer family. As highlighted in earlier chapters, Joan spent a good amount of time taking care of Bobby while their mother worked. It is likely that some of Joan's own needs—personally, academically, and socially—may have taken a back seat to the needs of Bobby and Regina. Joan's stress as a sometimes surrogate mother to Bobby becomes compounded when one consid-ers that there was no consistent father figure in the household, and the family was under constant financial strain. To be sure, the weighty re-sponsibility placed on Joan at an early age may have equipped her with skill sets that would serve her in later life—problem solving, lead-ership, coping and resilience; however, it is likely that Joan could have benefitted from personal counseling and support resources. There is now a significant body of research on the psychological development of the siblings of those with psychological and other challenges (Ehrenberg & Regev, 2011; Goeke & Ritchey, 2011; Lukens & Thorn-ing, 2011). Though these siblings are at times under great stress, they also develop coping and resilience skills. This research lends itself to developing psychoeducational and counseling support programs for siblings and families. Naturally, family counseling, though less popu-lar in the 1940s and 1950s than it is today, could have helped Bobby, Joan, and Regina as a family unit.

Psychological Intervention for Bobby Fischer

If the hypothesis posited in Chapter Seven is correct that Bobby Fischer may have suffered from a genetically predisposed Paranoid Personality Disorder, he could receive appropriate treatment, including long-term individual psychotherapy. Individuals suffering from Paranoid Personality Disorder are difficult patients for most therapists. This is understandable as such individuals often exhibit mistrust, antagonism, rigidity, and introversion, characteristics which challenge the critical "therapeutic alliance" between patient and therapist. Master clinicians have outlined challenges and strategies for therapeutic work with individuals who suffer from Paranoid Personality Disorder, and the interested reader is referred to these sources (Beck, Freeman, & Davis, 2004; Benjamin, 1996; O'Donohue, Fowler, & Lilienfeld, 2007; Millon et al., 2004; Shedler, 2009; Turkat, 1990).

With regard to schooling, Bobby would likely receive special support services, including individual and group counseling, which he probably did not receive at Public School 3 where he was expelled for a violent act (Targ, 2008), or at Erasmus high school where he voluntarily dropped out during his junior year. Depending on the presence and intensity of co-morbid (co-existing) symptoms such as anxiety, depression, and attention deficits in various subject areas, Bobby might be prescribed a psychotropic medication. Too little is known about Bobby's day-to-day behavior and affective state in elementary or high school to confidently recommend a particular medication regiment.

Though it is known that Bobby had a very ambivalent relationship with his mother, he could have benefitted from grief and support counseling in the 1997 and 1998 period when both his mother and sister passed away. If the hypothesis is correct that Bobby may have developed later in life (1990s) a delusional disorder to overlap a pre-existing paranoid personality disorder, than he may have benefitted from one of the newer anti-psychotic medications to attenuate the delusions. The newer, or atypical anti-psychotics work by blocking serotonin and dopamine (neurotransmitters) receptors in the brain. Sample drugs in this class of medication include Risperdol, Clozaril, and Zyprexa (Mental Health and Delusional Disorder, WEBMD, 2010). It is important that ongoing psychotherapy be in place in the treatment of Delusional Disorder. I remind my readers that I am only hypothesizing possible interventions for Bobby Fischer as a definitive diagnosis of his mental state was never conducted.

Would Bobby Fischer have become World Chess Champion if he had been involved in long-term individual psychotherapy, family therapy, special support services throughout his schooling, and possibly psychotropic medication (with their side effects)? This question I cannot answer. Perhaps these mental health interventions would have distracted Bobby from his chess focus and goals, and he would never have reached the world title. Psychotherapy usually aims to curb obsessions and promote balanced social, academic, vocational, and avocational activities. However, it was Bobby's obsession with the game of chess starting in childhood that launched him into his more than ten thousand hours of deliberate chess study that brought him to his elite skill level (refer back to Chapter Two on the role of deliberate study and practice in gaining chess mastery).

From the alternate perspective, it may be that long-term psychological interventions would have stabilized Bobby's personal life and his chess career. Psychoanalyst and Grandmaster, Dr. Reuben Fine (2008), who had met Bobby (and played chess with him) on a number of occasions believed that psychotherapy would have helped Bobby. Furthermore, Fischer's chief biographer, Dr. Frank Brady, who knew Bobby for decades also believed that psychotherapy would have benefitted Bobby personally and professionally (Frank Brady, personal communication, February 8, 2011).

Psychological treatment could have equipped Bobby with stress management and media-pressure management coping skills; it could have provided cognitive and behavioral techniques bringing his cognitive distortions and anti-Semitism under more control; it could have given him insight into his family history and the impact of not having a consistent father figure and perhaps not even knowing who his father was; it could have helped him cope with his mother's constant traveling and outspoken activism; and it could have supported him in developing and maintaining friendships and romantic partners. If this cadre of interventions were successful, even in part, Bobby Fischer might very well have been World Chess Champion for a decade or more, rather than for just three years. Interestingly, in a rigorous and carefully designed study on the relationship between age and skill level among 5,011 FIDE rated players (average ELO rating of 2,173), Roring and Charness (2007) found the peak skill rating to coincide with the age of 43.8 years, which is older than what had been previously thought. Clearly, Bobby Fischer, who basically withdrew from competition at the age of 29 (save for his 1992 comeback match against Spassky), had many years of elite chess ahead of him had he maintained his psychological health and competitive interests.

WHAT CAN BE LEARNED FROM THE BOBBY FISCHER STORY?

First, the Fischer story, from a mental health perspective, supports the diathesis stress model in psychology (Zuckerman, 1999). Individuals are born into this world with a genetic make-up (and therefore with personality and behavioral predispositions) passed down from parents and grandparents. Under the right mix of environmental circumstances, genetic predispositions will manifest themselves in particular thinking and behavior patterns. These could be positive, as in channeling a gift for memory and spatial relations into a defined task (i.e., chess), as well as negative, as in a tendency to be obsessive or distrustful of others. In Bobby Fischer's case, his genetic predispositions in concert with his early childhood environment and family dynamics (refer back to Chapter Three), manifested in both positive and negative behavioral and personality attributes. Naturally, implications here for mental health professionals are to conduct a comprehensive, sociocultural, multigeneration family assessment (see Grieger, 2008; Suzuki & Ponterotto, 2008, for examples from an interdisciplinary, sociocultural perspective) in the hopes of identifying and addressing both risk and resilience factors.

Second, the Bobby Fischer story speaks to the need to attend in early childhood to the psychological, academic, and social needs of gifted and talented youth. A challenge facing parents, coaches, and school counselors is how to promote a prodigy's specific gift, while also promoting balanced academic, social, and avocational interests. Parents of chess prodigies (as well as prodigies in other areas) are often torn between fostering and "pushing" the development of the gift in their children, versus promoting what is often labeled a "normal childhood" (see Hoffman, 2007, & Waitzkin, 1988 for revealing discussions on this topic).

I believe school counselors, and psychologists at all levels, can be more involved in proactive interventions targeted at the special needs of the talented and gifted in a variety of skill areas. There is an extensive research base on giftedness and the development of expertise (e.g., Ericsson, Charness, Feltovich, & Hoffman, 2006), and this research can guide the development of educational and prevention programs in schools aimed at children and their families. A first step is to be sure that school counseling training curriculum includes adequate attention to the study of gifted and talented children and their extended families.

Intervention programs for schools could include psychoeducational groups for children and their parents, group counseling for gifted children, group support programs for parents of gifted children, and role model and mentoring programs where children are matched with older, gifted classmates or community mentors. As research on expert performance indicates (Gladwell, 2008), it takes roughly 10,000 hours of deliberate study and practice to be an elite performer at a defined task (chess, math, ice skating, violin, and so forth). The question is, at what cost? What is lost in other areas of development when so much time is devoted to a singular pursuit? This is a topic for discussion among parents, grandparents and extended families, and for the students themselves. And it is best to address these questions early on in the families with gifted children.

EPILOGUE

Nothing is as healing as the human touch.
(Bobby Fischer's likely last words, spoken to friend Dr. Magnus
Skulason the night of his death, cited in Carlin, 2011, p. 7)

This book has combined three of my academic loves: psychology, biography, and chess. Working on this book the past few years has been challenging, exciting, and, at times poignant and moving. The challenge was in writing my first psychobiography. This form of writing and research was quite different than what I had been accustomed to in my 30 years of academic psychological research, which usually included large samples of participants but seldom a penetrating focus on an individual family. Psychobiography incorporates history, biography, and investigative journalism, and though I have always held an interest in these areas as a reader, writing in the area as a scholar necessitated focused study and some good mentoring (I discuss some of these mentors in the book "Acknowledgments" section). In effect, in my late mid-life (early 50s) I have taken on a new scholarly specialty: the intensive study of the individual life. In many ways, this work is more similar to how I think and work as a psychologist in private practice; and thus it feels comfortable and is consistent with my world view of understanding people.

Learning more about the chess world and Bobby Fischer's life was very exciting for me. As my American hero in the early 1970s, Bobby Fischer's genius and personality always fascinated me. After Bobby's impressive victory over Spassky in 1972, I had only followed his life from afar, but now, in committing to this book, I was able to intensely study Bobby's life from the lens of decades of work as a multicultural psychologist. Meeting in person or talking by phone and/or e-mail with individuals who knew Bobby well was riveting and exciting. Individuals such as Russell Targ, Anthony Saidy, Frank Brady, Robert Lipton, and for two fascinating meetings, William Lombardy, provided me with vivid images of Bobby's life that could not be gained by just reading about him. Thanks to kind introductions from chess ambassador Paul Albert, I also got to meet briefly other chess masters and grandmasters that are part of American and world chess history. In a way it has been like that "fantasy camp" where middle-aged men and women go to, and for a short time engage a passion with individuals who have lived that passion. Fortunately, my fantasy camp has now lasted four years, rather than the typical 1- or 2-week getaway.

My work the last few years has also been moving and poignant. When I began my research on Bobby Fischer, I did not really think about the personal relationships I would form as my work progressed. Extended family members of Bobby's, particularly his brother-in-law Russell Targ, and his niece's former boyfriend, Robert Lipton, trusted me with their stories and memories of Bobby and the Fischer family. I was and remain honored by this trust, and I hope that I have been respectful of the Fischer family and legacy in my writing. Likewise, close former friends of Bobby's, particularly Dr. Anthony Saidy and Dr. Frank Brady, provided me more mentoring, insight, and guidance than they likely could ever know. The same is said for journalists Clea Benson and Peter Nicholas who have served as a lighthouse, pointing me in proper directions for research, and guiding me in discoveries of critical connections in the Fischer story. I count all these individuals as new friends, though some of them I have not yet met in person.

What is the next chapter in the Bobby Fischer story? Intense interest in him and his life story will not wane; he is too fascinating as a historical figure to fade from the curiosity of chess players, biographers, historians, and psychologists. As with the chess legend Paul Morphy, who lived a century earlier, Bobby Fischer will continue to capture the world's imagination and puzzlement. It is likely that this book will generate mixed reactions in the chess world and beyond, as stories on Bobby Fischer invariably do. My hope is that this work generates continued scholarly interest in Bobby Fischer's life story. Though this book attempted to answer some lingering questions about Bobby's mental state, it left many more questions unresolved and has raised new areas for inquiry for psychologists, historians, and chess professionals.

Personally, I have been challenged and invigorated by my work on the Bobby Fischer story, and I plan to pursue different lines of both quantitative and qualitative research in fashioning a more comprehensive understanding of his life. I also hope to use the knowledge and insight I have gained in studying the life of Bobby Fischer to be a more sensitive, competent, and impactful psychologist when working with elite chess players, other gifted and talented individuals, as well as those at some psychological risk. To my readers, I thank you for taking this journey with me; and I hope that you have found this book of some value. Now back to chess.

NOTES

Chapter Two

1. Though Bobby Fischer was the first "official" World Chess Champion from the United States, most chess experts and historians consider New Orleans' born and raised Paul Morphy to be this country's first world champion. Morphy was considered the best player in the World in the 1858–1859 time period when he defeated most of Europe's best players. However, the title of "official" world champion was not used until the time of Wilhelm Steinitz in 1886. Paul Morphy's life and chess career is discussed at length in Chapter Eight.
2. The United States Chess Federation (USCF) grew substantially in the 1990s and 2000s due to scholastic memberships. Given the low membership fee for scholastic youth this led to some financial strain on the organization. At present, USCF membership has scaled back and stands at about 80,000 which appears to be sustainable financially for the organization.
3. Though no United States Champion captivated the country like Bobby Fischer when he won eight U.S. titles, there have been great and repeat North American Champions. Among the multiyear U.S. Champions since 1972 are Walter Browne, Yasser Seirawan, Alexander Shabalov, Nick de Firmian, Gata Kamsky, and Hikaru Nakamura, among others. On the world stage, Hikaru Nakamura (ELO = 2758) and Gata Kamsky (ELO = 2756) are the most competitive internationally and rank among the top 15 players in the world (as of September, 2011).

Chapter Three

1. The extensive FBI files on Regina Fischer do document limited mail correspondence between Gerhard and Regina Fischer soon after Regina and Joan Fischer's entry into the United States in 1939. It is also known from these files that Joan traveled to Chile in young adulthood to spend time with her father. Joan's surviving husband, Russell Targ, also discussed this travel in his autobiography (Targ, 2008).
2. Reuben Fine was among the top two chess players in the world when he tied for first place with Keres in the famed 1938 AVRO tournament. He and Keres finished ahead of Botvinnik, Euwe, Reshevsky, Alekhine, Capablanca, and Flohr.

Reuben Fine also became a world renowned psychoanalyst and author in New York City after retiring from competitive chess. He earned his Ph.D. in Psychology from the University of Southern California in 1948 where his dissertation research was on "The Personality of the Asthmatic Child." I had the privilege of a meeting with Richard D. Ross, Ph.D., of New York City who was an acquaintance of Dr. Fine's in his later years. Dr. Ross provided me valuable insights into the personality and family life of Reuben Fine.

Chapter Four

1. According to FBI documents (# 100–102290), Gerardo Fischer arrived at Los Andes, Chile on January 4, 1940. He held a Spanish passport and had obtained Spanish citizenship in 1938. As of October, 1945 he was living in Santiago, Chile and was self-employed as a photographer. The FBI report goes on to state that he "was a member of the Communist Party (CP) and associated with numerous pro-communist individuals." The FBI believed Gerardo may have been a Soviet spy monitoring the activity of German expatriates living in Chile.
2. In my discussions with Russell Targ, Regina's son-in-law, who knew Regina quite well from roughly 1957 until Regina's death in 1997 (see Targ, 2008), he cautioned me not to pay attention to her psychiatric report as he believed it to be inaccurate. Though Mr. Targ is not a mental health professional trained in psychological assessment, he is a well-informed scientist and the person currently alive who knew Regina Fischer best.
3. The exact circumstances regarding why Regina Fischer moved out of the 560 Lincoln Place, Brooklyn apartment are unclear. Did Regina decide to leave or did Bobby ask Regina to leave? Regardless of who initiated Regina's departure from Brooklyn for the Bronx, the fact is that at the young age of 17, Bobby Fischer was pretty much on his own.
4. Various theories of psychology and psychotherapy hold that the life of one's ancestors filters down psychologically to impact one's development and one's way of being in the world. Carl Jung's (1968) "collective unconscious" is a good example from the psychodynamic and psychoanalytic literature. Eduardo Duran's (2010) concept of ancestral connectedness is very prevalent in models of multicultural and Native American indigenous psychology (Ponterotto, 2010). Duran believes that all humans are interconnected by seven generations past as well as seven generations yet to come.
5. New Jersey State Law allows researchers to access the "Certificate and Record of Death" for informational purposes (that is not for legal or estate matters) for persons deceased at least 40 years. In New York, the waiting period is 50 years. Researchers should check the laws and regulations of the particular state of interest when conducting genealogical research.
6. The U.S. Federal Census data for New Jersey State Psychiatric Hospital at Greystone Park (Morris Plains, N.J.) documents Natalie Wender's residence there in 1920. Natalie's native language and country of birth, however, are listed erroneously as German and Bavaria, respectively. More accurate information on

Natalie's demographic background is on her death certificate, which also documents her death at New Jersey State Hospital at Greystone.

7. As noted earlier in this chapter, Regina Fischer had informed her family that her mother Natalie had died in the 1918 flu pandemic. It is not known how long Natalie's psychiatric symptoms were present before her hospitalization at the New Jersey State Psychiatric facility. Further, it is not known if the hospitalization was voluntary or through an involuntary commitment order (the Greystone psychiatric records are confidential). Although there was a spike in encephalitis lethargica in the years following the 1918 flu pandemic, there is little empirical evidence that the flu caused or potentiated neurological damage in a person who caught but survived the flu; however, this possibility cannot be ruled out (McCall, Vilensky, Gilman, & Taubenberger, 2008). The probability is, however, that Natalie Wender exhibited psychiatric symptoms prior to the 1918 flu pandemic and that the flu did not cause neurological damage leading to a psychiatric disorder. In addition to the important work of McCall et al. (2008) on the possible relationship between the 1918 flu and encephalitis lethargic, an important source of information on the nature and procedures for psychiatric hospitalizations (and the nature of the patients) in the late 1800s and early 1900s is provided by Penney and Stastny's (2008) *The Lives Left Behind.* An excellent overview of the 1918 flu pandemic is provided in Crosby's (2003), *America's Forgotten Pandemic: The influenza of 1918.*

8. On the original birth certificate of Gerhardt Fischer, no name for the boy is given. However, on a handwritten addition placed on the right side of the birth certificate, his decided name as Hans Gerhardt Joachim (Liebscher Fischer) was added. This addition to the birth record was made on October 26, 1908.

Chapter Six

1. It should be noted that at times Mikkail Tal and Bobby Fischer had a mutually respectful relationship, and Bobby visited Tal in the hospital during a tournament in Curacao. Dr. Anthony Saidy, an International Chess Master who knew Tal and Fischer, reported to me that Tal was a beloved person who often joked and played around, and that he would not have likely insulted Bobby as implied in the Solotaroff (1992) article (Dr. Anthony Saidy, personal communication, October 14, 2011).

Chapter Eight

1. Though David Lawson is often credited with the moniker "The Pride and Sorrow of Chess," he acknowledged that he borrowed the phrase from the Walter C. Spens (1892) sonnet in the *Glasgow Weekly Herald.*

2. Challenges in staffing and running the institution led Bishop Portier to recruit French Jesuit priests from Lyon, France to take over the institution, which they did in 1847. The first Jesuit president was Francis de S. Gautrelet, S.J. (serving from 1847–1859), and he was president during the matriculations of both Edward (1848–1852) and Paul Morphy (1850–1855). Since the leadership of Fr. Gautrelet,

there have been 24 Presidents of Spring Hill College, and all have been Jesuit priests (Spring Hill Home Page, April 2, 2011).

3. In reading an earlier version of this chapter, noted historian Thomas Aiello remarked that though it was true that Paul Morphy was multilingual, such linguistic competence was not uncommon or rare among New Orleans society in the mid-1800s.

4. Historian Thomas Aiello, in responding to this chapter, believed that Morphy's stance against forcible secession likely had little to do with his law career failures, believing instead that his career disappointments had more to do with his typecast image as a chess champion.

5. My check of historical weather records showed that the average high temperature in New Orleans during the month of July is 91 degrees Fahrenheit.

6. Fischer biographer Dr. Frank Brady relayed the following story to me during our e-mail correspondence. Brady had taken Bobby to dinner at the home of Morphy biographer David Lawson in Brooklyn. Lawson had a bust of Paul Morphy's hands, and when Bobby placed his hands on top of the bust his hands completely engulfed Morphy's hands as if an adult cupping a child's hands.

Chapter Nine

1. According to the Substance Abuse and Mental Health Services Administration (SAMHSA), "serious mental illness" is defined as "persons aged 18 or older who currently or at any time in the past year have a diagnosable mental, behavioral, or emotional disorder (excluding developmental and substance use disorder) of sufficient duration to meet diagnostic criteria specified within the 4th edition of the *Diagnostic and Statistical Manual of mental Disorders* (*DSM-IV*) (American Psychiatric Association [APA], 1994) that has resulted in serious functional impairment, which substantially interferes with or limits one or more major life activities." Whereas the category of "any mental illness" is applied regardless of the level of functional impairment (U.S. Department of Health and Human Services, 2009, pp. 7 and 9).

2. Other studies supporting these national incidence rates include the following: Dewa, Lesage, Goering, & Caveen, 2004; Fichter et al., 1996; Grant et al., 2009; Kessler et al., 2001; Kessler & Wang, 2008; Narrow, Rae, Robins, & Regier, 2002; and Regier et al., 1993; all of which are included in the book's reference section.

APPENDICES

Appendix A

SELECT CHESS ACHIEVEMENTS OF BOBBY FISCHER

1949 – At the age of 6, Fischer begins playing chess.

1952 – By the age of 9, Fischer's commitment to chess is solidified, and he begins to exhibit special talent for the game.

1956 – At the age of 13 wins the U.S. Junior Chess Championship; designated a Chess Master; in a game against Donald Byrne at the Rosenwald Memorial tournament in New York City, wins the brilliancy prize in a performance dubbed "Game of the Century."

1958 – At the age of 14 wins the U.S. Chess Championship; receives title of International Master.

1958 – By placing fifth in the Interzonal Tournament in Portoroz, Yugoslavia, Bobby is designated an International Grandmaster.

1958–1965 – Fischer wins 8 consecutive U.S. Chess Championships in which he participates.

1966 – Co-authored *Bobby Fischer Teaches Chess* (one of the word's best-selling chess books [see Chun, 2002].

1969 – His book *My 60 Memorable Games* was published by Simon & Schuster and is considered a classic in the field (see Chun, 2002).

1970 – Wins Interzonal Tournament in Palma de Majorca, Spain ahead of 23 of the world's most eminent chess players.

1971 – Defeats Mark Taimanov 6–0 in Candidates Match in Vancouver, Canada.

1971 – Defeats Bent Larsen 6–0 in Candidates match in Denver, Colorado.

1971 – Defeats Tigran Petrosian $6\frac{1}{2}$–$2\frac{1}{2}$ in Buenos Aires, Argentina, and earns right to challenge Boris Spassky for the World Title.

1972 – Fischer becomes world chess champion after defeating Russian Boris Spassky in Reykjavik, Iceland in convincing fashion $12\frac{1}{2}$–$8\frac{1}{2}$.

1992 – Fischer again defeats Boris Spassky in an unsanctioned (by FIDE or any other Chess Organization) rematch in Yugoslavia.

Appendix B

SELECT PERSONAL CHALLENGES AND EVENTS IN BOBBY FISCHER'S LIFE

1949 – Bobby is expelled from Public School 3 in New York City for kicking its principal, Mr. Sallen (Targ, 2008, and personal communication July 20, 2010).

1952 – March 1, Bobby's likely biological father, Dr. Paul Nemenyi dies while at a dance at the International Student House, 1825 R. Street, NW, Washington, DC. Pronounced dead at 9:57 p.m. of natural causes by a Dr. Claudey (FBI document # 65–45667-64).

1957 – On a car trip with other chess players from Milwaukee to Long Beach, California, Bobby bites Gil Ramirez during a fight in the back seat of the car; the bite mark was still visible in 2000 according to Fischer former friend and Chess Master, Ron Gross (Franett, 2000, p. 2).

1959 – Dropped out of Erasmus High School (Brooklyn, New York) at 16 years of age.

1961 – In an interview with Ralph Ginzburg, Bobby reveals seeds of anti-Semitism that would grow virulent and paranoid over the next decades (Ginzburg, 1962).

1962 – Bobby gets into a fistfight with Pal Benko while in Stockholm; years later Benko stated "I am sorry that I beat up Bobby. He was a sick man, even then (see Brady, 2011, p. 146).

1964 – Bobby fails his military draft physical examination (Brady, 1973).

1971 – While living with his sister Joan's family (husband Russell Targ, and children Elisabeth, Nicholas, and Alexander) in Northern California, Bobby is asked to move out because of his anti-semitic attitudes and comments (Russell Targ, personal communication, July 20, 2010).

1974 – Bobby sues author Brad Darrach for an unfavorable portrayal of Bobby in *Bobby Fischer vs. Rest of the World;* Bobby loses the suit.

1975 – The World Chess Federation stripped Bobby of his world title for refusal to play Anatoly Karpov who had earned the right to challenge him.

1975 – Bobby sues the Worldwide Church of God and loses.

1976 – Fischer reportedly assaults an ex-member of the Worldwide Church of God he felt had violated his confidence; Fischer was sued and settled the suit (Solotaroff, 1992).

1977 – Bobby cuts ties to Worldwide Church of God.

1981 – Bobby arrested in Pasadena, CA and held for roughly 48 hours (he was wandering the streets and was questioned by police because he fit a description of a bank robber; he did not cooperate with police during initial questioning and was arrested). He later wrote and self-published a 14-page pamphlet: "I was tortured in the Pasadena Jailhouse" (Fischer, 1982).

1992 – In playing Boris Spassky in 1992 in Yugoslavia, Bobby violated U.S. sanctions and an arrest warrant was issued by the U.S. State Department.

2000 – There are some reports that Bobby and companion, Marilyn Young, had a baby daughter named Jinky Young in the Philippines (Weber, 2008).

2004 – Bobby was seized by Japanese authorities for an invalid passport when he tried to board a plane for Manila. He was detained for nine months.

2008 – Bobby Fischer passes away on January 17 at the age of 64 (reportedly of kidney failure). Until the very end he refused medical treatment (Targ, 2008).

2010 – Bobby's body is exhumed on July 5th to resolve a paternity suit claim brought on by Justine Young, his possible daughter with Marilyn Young; the DNA match is negative; Bobby is not the biological father.

2011 – Reykjavik courts move that Miyoko Watai is legally Bobby's wife and she is sole inheritor of Bobby's estate.

Appendix C

REGINA FISCHER TIMELINE

1913 – Born in Zurich, Switzerland (March 31) to Jacob Wender and Natalie (Abramson) Wender (FBI Report # CG: 100–27015).

1913 – Regina's father, Jacob Wender arrives at Ellis Island, New York on August 5, aboard the SS Zeeland; he had departed Antwerp on July 26, 1913. He is passenger #4 on the ship's manifest and reports being 29 years of age.

1914 – Regina, her brother Max, and her mother Natalie arrive in the United States.

1920 – While Regina's mother, Natalie Wender is a patient at the New Jersey State Psychiatric Hospital at Greystone Park, Morris Plains, NJ, Regina and Max are placed in the Brooklyn Hebrew Orphanage Asylum in Kings County, Brooklyn, NY.

1921 – Regina's mother, Natalie Wender, dies.

1923 – Regina's father marries Ethel Greenberg in St. Louis, when Regina is 10 years old.

1925 – Regina runs away from home but subsequently returns (FBI Report # CG: 100–27015).

1926 – November 12th, Regina becomes a Naturalized Citizen of the United States; her father Jacob Wender is residing at 270 South Third Street, Brooklyn, New York.

1928 – While in high school (late 1920s) Regina does not live with father and stepmother, but with friends (not identified) (FBI Report # CG: 100–27015).

1929 – Regina graduates from Soldon High School in St. Louis; she is only 15 years of age.

1930 – According to the U.S. Decennial Census of 1930, Regina is living in St. Louis, Missouri with father Jacob Wender, stepmother Ethel (Greenberg) Wender, brother Max, and stepsister Sylvia.

1932 – Withdraws from the University of Colorado for financial reasons and because of desire to travel (FBI Report # CG: 100–27015).

1932 – Travels to Europe and visits brother who is enlisted with U.S. Navy and stationed in Germany. Subsequently takes a job with a university in Berlin where she meets future husband, a German physicist, Hans Gerhardt Fischer (FBI Report # CG: 100–27015).

1933 – Student at the First Moscow Medical Institute (1933–1938) (Brady, 2011).

1933 – November 4th, Regina marries Hans Gerhardt (Gerardo) Fischer (Liebscher) in Moscow, Russia.

1937 – July 8th, gives birth to daughter Joan in Moscow, Russia.

1937 – Regina's father Jacob Wender and his wife Ethel Greenberg divorce

1938 – Moves to Paris with Joan and finds employment as an English teacher (at some point husband Hans Gerhardt Fischer joins them in Paris) (Brady, 2011).

1939 – January 23rd, Regina and Joan return to United States without Gerhardt, and settle in New York until sometime in 1940 (FBI Reports # CG 100–27015 and NY 100–102290).

1940 – Meets Paul Nemenyi while at the University of Denver (FBI Report # NY 100–102290).

1942 – Moves to Sioux City, Iowa for employment as a civil service (government) worker (FBI Report # CG 100–27015).

1943 – While pregnant, Regina moves to Chicago; she tells case worker she moved to Chicago because of its reputation for excellent maternal conditions at Michael Reese Hospital (FBI Report # CG: 100–27015).

1942 – October, FBI surveillance of Regina Fischer begins.

1943 – Regina gives birth "to a boy named NEMENYI" (FBI Report # NY 100–102290, p. 24). Of course this is Bobby Fischer.

1943 – (June 21st) Arrested in Chicago on charge of disturbing peace (Court case # 4795013). Received psychiatric evaluation on 6/22/1943 by the Chicago Municipal Psychiatric Institute; received diagnosis of "stilted (paranoid) personality, querulent, but not psychotic" (FBI Report # CG: 100–27015).

1944 – Summer months, Regina, Joan, and Bobby live in Pullman, Washington (in an apartment rented by Paul Nemenyi who visits the family regularly) (FBI Report # CG 100–27015).

1944 – Regina's father marries Ethel Greenberg again, this time in New York City.

1945 – Regina is recruited to join Communist Party Association in Oregon.

1945 – September 14th, while living in Moscow, Idaho, Regina divorces Hans Gerhardt Fischer on grounds of "willful neglect." The case is handled by attorneys Louis Huff in Moscow, Idaho, and Peter Pfeffer in Santiago, Chile.

1946 – Regina first contacts Jewish Family Service (JFS; located at 113 West 57th Street, New York City) for support. This was the first of multiple contacts with JFS in various cities. FBI documents indicate other contacts in 1948, 1951, 1957, and 1958).

1946 – Regina moves to Los Angeles, works as a public school teacher and also works in the L.A. County Coroner's Office (FBI Report # NY 100–102290).

1947 – Paul Nemenyi joins Regina and Bobby in Los Angeles, however, he later reports to Jewish Family Services that Regina was very hostile toward him forcing him to leave Los Angeles.

1948 – Regina returns to New York City with Joan and Bobby (FBI Report # NY

100–102290).

1948 – Regina obtains employment in New York, places Bobby in Joan's care while she homeschools both (length of this is uncertain) (FBI Report # NY 100–102290).

1955 – Regina's father Jacob Wender and his wife Ethel Greenberg divorce for a second time.

1958 – Regina is working as a Private Duty nurse affiliated with the Nursing Bureau of District 14, Brooklyn, NY.

1961 – In July, Regina leaves her apartment at 560 Lincoln Place in Brooklyn and moves to 1804 Longfellow Avenue, Bronx, New York; Bobby retains apartment.

1973 – January 24th, Regina is arrested in Paris, France for carrying two placards that read "Nixon, No More Delay, Sign Today," and " I am an American, Mr. Nixon End the Vietnam War." The police take her to the police station at 43 bis rue Taitbout, Paris.

1997 – Regina (Wender) Fischer (Pustan) dies of cancer in Palo Alto, California.

Appendix D

PAUL MORPHY TIMELINE

1837 – Born June 22, in New Orleans.

1841 – Morphy families moves from home at 1113 Chartres Street to 89 Royal Street (now 417 Royal Street).

1843 – First record of his chess-playing prowess vividly described by his best friend, Charles Maurian, in a New Orleans newspaper some 65 years after the incident.

1846 – Defeats General Winfield Scott in 2 games publicly witnessed.

1849 – At 12 years of age defeats strong chess player Eugene Rousseau.

1850 – Defeats world-renowned chess player, Johann J. Lowenthal, a political refugee from Hungary visiting New Orleans.

1850 – Graduates from Jefferson Academy in New Orleans.

1850 – Enters Spring Hill College.

1854 – Receives A.B. degree from Spring Hill College.

1855 – Receives A.M. degree from Spring Hill College.

1856 – Alonzo Morphy, Paul's father dies of apoplexy or congestion of the brain, and leaves an estate valued at $146,162.54.

1857 – Receives law degree, L.L.B. from University of Louisiana.

1857 – Wins the Grand Tournament at the First Congress of the American National Chess Association, New York; considered United States Champion; stays in New York for three months, departing for New Orleans on December 17th.

1858 – May 31st departs New Orleans for England (passing through New York) on way to England for European challenges, particularly to play Howard Staunton, the renowned English champion; arrives in Liverpool on June 20th and then London on June 21st.

1858 – On June 23rd or 24th, visits Staunton's country home in Streatham with established English players Thomas W. Barnes and Reverend John Owen. Staunton refuses a game with Morphy, but agrees to two "consultation" (team games) where Staunton teams with Owen and Morphy with Barnes. Morphy's team wins both games. This would be the only known encounter between Morphy and Staunton.

1858 – July and August, Morphy again beats Lowenthal in 14 game match in

London, winning nine, losing three, and drawing two.

1858 – September and October, Morphy defeats David Harrwitz (who had previously defeated Lowenthal) in an eight game match in Paris with five wins, two losses, and one draw.

1858 – September 15, Morphy has first sitting with French sculptor Eugene Lequesne for marble bust, considered by Charles Maurian and others to be the best likeness of Morphy ever sculpted.

1858 – December, Morphy defeats German champion, Adolf Anderssen (who had won the famed International Chess Congress tournament of 1851 held in London, and was therefore considered the Champion of all of Europe) with seven wins, two losses, and two draws. At the age of twenty-two Morphy is now heralded internationally as the World Champion of Chess.

1859 – April 6th, Morphy heads back to New Orleans (stopping in England and New York City); his brother-in-law John Sybrandt (who figures prominently in Morphy's mental illness later) arrives in Paris to facilitate, ensure, and hasten his departure from Europe.

1859 – In July, Morphy sits for an oil portrait by Charles Loring Elliott, which now hangs in the Manhattan Chess Club, New York City.

1860 – Louisiana becomes the sixth state (of an eventual eleven) to vote to secede from the union.

1861 – Morphy travels to Richmond, VA and meets with General P.G.T. Beauregard of the Confederacy who was originally from New Orleans and knew the Morphy family.

1862 – In October, traveling with lifelong friend Charles Maurian, Morphy leaves New Orleans for Paris where his mother and sister Helena were waiting out the Civil War (Union troops occupied New Orleans since April). Morphy and Maurian stop over in Havana, Cuba and Cardiz, Spain enroute to Paris arriving in December.

1864 – In January, very concerned over state of affairs at home, Morphy leaves Paris, landing in Havana on February 16th and then in New Orleans in the last week of February.

1864 – Morphy sets up law practice in New Orleans.

1865 – Though not playing much chess (occasionally with friends), he accepts election as President of the New Orleans Chess Club (close friend Charles Maurian is elected secretary).

1867 – Law practice does not seem to be going well; mother is concerned with Morphy's increasing melancholy and general social withdrawal (except for opera of which he was a confirmed lover), and mother persuades him to return to Paris with herself and Paul's sister Helena. Morphy remains in Paris for fifteen months, returning to the United States (first New York) in September, 1868.

1875 – Signs of Morphy's psychological deterioration (persecutory delusions) are first acknowledged and described by close friend Charles Maurian. Family members take Paul to the "Louisiana Retreat," and institution for the insane run by Catholic nuns, but Morphy refuses admittance and is taken home.

1879 – Anecdotal reports of Morphy's delusional and odd behavior appear with increasing frequency.

1879 – Plays his last games of chess against friend Charles Maurian.

1883 – Meets with Wilhelm Steinitz (who would become the world's first official world champion, 1886 through 1894). While Steinitz is visiting New Orleans for a month, the two talk but do not play chess. Interestingly, Steinitz would experience delusions in 1896 and 1900 and was hospitalized (briefly) for mental illness.

1884 – Dies while taking a cool bath after a walk on a hot day; he had apparently been in good health.

REFERENCES

Aiello, T. (Ed.). (2009). *Dan Burley's jive*. DeKalb, IL: Northern Illinois University Press.

Aiello, T. (2011). *Bayou classic: The Grambling-Southern football rivalry*. Baton Rouge, LA: Louisiana State University Press.

Aiello, T. (2010). Editor's introduction. In D. Lawson's *Paul Morphy: The pride and sorrow of chess* (New Edition, pp. ix–xxvi). Lafayette, LA: University of Louisiana at Lafayette Press.

Aiello, T. (2011). *The kings of casino park: Race and race baseball in the lost season of 1932*. Tuscaloosa, AL: University of Alabama Press.

Albert, P. M., Jr. (2004). Foreword. In D. Kopec & L. Ftacnik's *Winning the won game: Lessons from the Albert brilliancy prizes* (pp. 5–10). New York: Batsford.

Albert, P. M., Jr. (2009). *My contacts with Robert James ("Bobby") Fischer*. Unpublished memoir section. New York, NY.

American Mathematical Monthly. (1944). News and Notes. *The American Mathematical Monthly, 51*(2), 104–108.

American Mathematical Monthly. (1947). Annual Meeting of the Illinois Section. *The American Mathematical Monthly, 54*(6), 361–363.

American Mental Health Counseling Association (AMHCA). (2010). *Code of ethics*. Alexandria, VA: American Mental Health Counseling Association.

American Psychiatric Association. (1994). *Diagnostic and statistical manual of mental disorders* (4th ed.). Washington, DC: Author.

American Psychiatric Association. (2000). *Diagnostic and statistical manual of mental disorders* (4th ed. text revision). Washington, DC: Author.

American Psychological Association. (2002). *Ethical principles of psychologists and code of conduct*. Washington, DC: Author.

Anand, V. (2008). *He (Fischer) and Kasparov were the greatest in history, but I judge Kasparov as a little ahead*. Chessbase.com, February 15.

Andreasen, N. C. (1987). Creativity and mental illness: Prevalence rates in writers and their first-degree relatives. *American Journal of Psychiatry, 144*, 1288–1292.

Anything to win: The mad genius of Bobby Fischer. (2004). Documentary Film, executive producers Stephen Land, Geoffrey Proud, & Peter Tarshis. New York: Jupiter Entertainment for A&E Television Network and Biography Channel.

Beck, A. T., Freeman, A., & Davis, D. D., & Associates. (2004). *Cognitive therapy of personality disorders* (2nd ed.). New York: Guilford.

Benjamin, L. S. (1996). *Interpersonal diagnosis and treatment of personality disorders*. New York: Guilford.

Benson, H. (2011). *Bobby Fischer*. Brooklyn, NY: Powerhouse Cultural Entertainment, Inc. (Compilation; photographs and text by Harry Benson).

Bilalic, M., Kiesel, A., Pohl, C., Erb, M., & Grodd, W. (2011). It takes two-skilled recognition of objects engages lateral areas in both hemispheres. *PLos ONE, 6* (1): e16202. Doi: 10.1371/journal.pone.0016202.

Bilalic, M., McLeod, P., & Gobet, F. (2007a). Does chess need intelligence?–A study with young chess players. *Intelligence, 35,* 457–470.

Bilalic, M., McLeod, P., & Gobet, F. (2007b). Personality profiles of young chess players. *Personality and Individual Differences, 42,* 901–910.

Bobby Fischer against the world. (2011). Documentary Film, executive producer Liz Garbus. New York: HBO Documentary Films.

Bohm, H., & Jongkind, K. (2003). *Bobby Fischer: The wandering king.* London: Batsford.

Brady, F. (1965). *Bobby Fischer: Profile of a prodigy.* New York: Dover.

Brady, F. (1973). *Bobby Fischer: Profile of a prodigy* (2nd ed.). New York: Dover.

Brady, F. (2004). Documentary Interview in *Anything to win: The mad genius of Bobby Fischer* (2004). Documentary Film, executive producers Stephen Land, Geoffrey Proud, & Peter Tarshis. New York: Jupiter Entertainment for A&E Television Network and Biography Channel.

Brady, F. (2011). *Endgame: The spectacular rise and fall of Bobby Fischer.* New York: Crown.

Buck, C. A. (1902). *Paul Morphy: His later life.* Newport, KY: Will. H. Lyons.

Campitelli, G., & Gobet, F. (2008). The role of practice in chess: A longitudinal study. *Learning and Individual Differences, 18,* 446–458.

Carlin, J. (2011). The end game of Bobby Fischer. *The Guardian/The Observer,* February 9, pp. 1–8.

Carson, S. H., Peterson, J. B., & Higgins, D. M. (2003). Decreased latent inhibition is associated with increased creative achievement in high-functioning individuals. *Journal of Personality and Social Psychology, 85,* 499–506.

Caspi, J. (Ed.). (2011). *Sibling development: Implications for mental health practitioners.* New York: Springer.

Charness, N., Tuffiash, M., Krampe, R., Reingold, E., & Vasyukova, E. (2005). The role of deliberate practice in chess expertise. *Applied Cognitive Psychology, 19,* 151–165.

Chun, R. (2002). Bobby Fischer's pathetic endgame. *The Atlantic Monthly, December,* 80–100.

Coolidge, F. L., Thede, L. L., & Jang, K. L. (2001). Heritability of personality disorders in childhood: A preliminary investigation. *Journal of Personality Disorders, 15,* 33–40.

Crosby, A. W. (2003). *America's forgotten pandemic: The influenza of 1918* (New edition). Cambridge, UK: Cambridge University Press.

Darrach, B. (2009). *Bobby Fischer vs. the rest of the world.* Oakland, CA: Ishi Press.

Dean, G., & Brady, M. (2010). *Chess masterpieces: One thousand years of extraordinary chess sets.* New York: Abrams.

Dean, S. B., & Targ, N. (Co-editors). (2006). *Human Rights, 33*(2), Spring Issue.

De Bruin, A. B. H., Smits, N., Rikers, R. M. J., & Schmidt, H. G. (2008). Deliberate practice predicts performance over time in adolescent chess players and drop-outs: A linear mixed model analysis. *British Journal of Psychology, 99,* 473–497.

de Manzano, O., Cervenka, S., Karabanov, A., Farde, L., & Ullen, F. (2010). Thinking outside a less intact box: Thalamic dopamine D2 receptor densities are negatively related to psychometric creativity in healthy individuals. *PLoS One, 5*(5): E10670. Doi:10.1371/journal.pone.0010670.

Denker, A., & Parr, L. (2009). *The Bobby Fischer I knew and other stories.* New York: Ishi Press International (First printing 1995, San Francisco: Hypermodern Press).

Dewa, C. S., Lesage, A., Goering, P., & Caveen, M. (2004). *HealthcarePapers, 5,* 12–25.

Dewa, C. S., & Lin, E. (2000). Chronic physical illness, psychiatric disorder and disability in the workplace. *Social Science & Medicine, 51,* 41–50.

Dresden, A. (1942). The migration of mathematicians. *American Mathematical Monthly, 49*(7), 415–429.

Duran, E. (2006). *Healing the soul wound: Counseling with American Indians and other native peoples.* New York: Teachers College (Columbia University) Press.

Ebert, B. W. (1987). Guide to conducting a psychological autopsy. *Professional Psychology: Research and Practice, 18,* 52–56.

Edge, F. M. (1859). *The exploits and triumphs in Europe of Paul Morphy.* New York: D. Appleton & Co.

Edmonds, D., & Eidinow, J. (2004). *Bobby Fischer goes to war: How a lone American star defeated the soviet chess machine.* New York: P.S.™ a trademark of HarperCollins.

Ehrenberg, M. F., & Regev, R. (2011). Sibling relationships in divorcing families. In J. Caspi (Ed.), *Sibling development: Implications for mental health practitioners* (pp. 273–288). New York: Springer.

Elms, A. C. (1994). *Uncovering lives: The uneasy alliance of biography and psychology.* New York: Oxford University Press.

Elo, A. (1986). *The rating of chess players, past and present* (2nd ed.). New York: Arco.

Ericsson, K. A., Charness, N., Feltovich, P. J., & Hoffman, R. R. (Eds.). (2006). *The Cambridge handbook of expertise and expert performance.* Cambridge, UK: Cambridge University Press.

Erikson, E. H. (1950). *Childhood and society.* New York: Norton.

Evans, L. (2003). *FBI files on Fischer.* Bobbyfischer.net, p. 1.

Evans, L. (2008). *The Bobby Fischer that we loved.* January 22, 2008, http://blog.chess.com/ttiot/.

Farkashazy, T. (2008). *Bobby Visszater avagy a Fischer-rejtely.* Published in Hungarian.

Fichter, M. M., Narrow, W. E., Roper, M. T., Rehm, J., Elton, M., Rae, D. S., Locke, B. Z., & Regier, D. A. (1996). Prevalence of mental illness in Germany and the United States. Comparison of the Upper Bavarian study and the epidemiologic catchment area program. *Journal of Nervous Mental Disorders, 184,* 598–606.

Fine, R. (2008). *Bobby Fischer's conquest of the world's championship: The psychology and tactics of the title match.* New York: Ishi Press. [Original printed in 1973, New York: David McKay.]

Fine, R. (2009). *The psychology of the chess player.* New York: Ishi Press International. (First published in 1956 as Psychoanalytic observations on chess and chess masters, by the National Psychological Association for Psychoanalysis.)

Fischer, B. (1982). *I was tortured in the Pasadena jailhouse.* Self-published by Bobby Fischer.

Franett, M. (2000). *The wanderer: The man who knew Bobby Fischer.* Bobbyfischer.net, pp. 1–5.

Ginzburg, R. (1962). Portrait of a genius as a young chess master. *Harper's Magazine, 224,* 1340 (January), pp. 49–55.

Gladwell, M. (2008). *Outliers: The story of success.* New York: Little, Brown and Company.

Gobet, F., & Charness, N. (2006). Expertise in chess. In K. A. Ericsson, N. Charness, P. J. Feltovich, & R. R. Hoffman (Eds.), *The Cambridge handbook of expertise and expert performance* (pp. 523–538). Cambridge, UK: Cambridge University Press.

Goeke, J., & Ritchey, K. D. (2011). Siblings of individuals with disabilities. In J. Caspi (Ed.), *Sibling development: Implications for mental health practitioners* (pp. 167–193). New York: Springer.

Grabner, R. H., Stern, E., & Neubauer, A. C. (2007). Individual differences in chess expertise: A psychometric investigation. *Acta Psychologica, 124,* 398–420.

Grant, B. F., Goldstein, R. B., Chou, S. P., Huang, B., Stinson, F. S., Dawson, D. A., Saha, T. D., Smith, S. M., Pulay, A. J., Pickering, R. P., Ruan, W. J., & Compton, W. M. (2009). Sociodemographic and psychopathologic predictors of first incidence of *DSM-IV* substance use, mood and anxiety disorders: Results from the wave 2 national epidemiologic survey on alcohol and related conditions. *Molecular Psychiatry, 14,* 1051–1066.

Grieger, I. (2008). A cultural assessment framework and interview protocol. In L. A. Suzuki & J. G. Ponterotto (Eds.), *Handbook of multicultural assessment: Clinical, psychological and educational applications* (3rd ed., pp. 132–161). San Francisco: Jossey-Bass.

Grieger, I., & Greene, P. (1998). The psychological autopsy as a tool in student affairs. *Journal of College Student Development, 39,* 388–392.

Hesse, M., & Thylstrup, B. (2008). Inter-rater agreement of comorbid DSM-IS personality disorders in substance abusers. *BMC Psychiatry (open access), 8*(37), 1–6.

Hill, B. E., & Wolfson, S., & Targ, N. (2004). Human rights and the environment: A synopsis and some predictions. *The Georgetown International Environmental Law Review, 16*(3), 359–402.

Hoffman, P. (2007). *King's gambit: A son, a father, and the world's most dangerous game.* New York: Hyperion.

Howard, R. W. (2005). Objective evidence of rising population ability: A detailed examination of longitudinal chess data. *Personality and Individual Differences, 38,* 347–363.

Howard, R. W. (2008). Linking extreme precocity and adult eminence: A study of eight prodigies at international chess. *High Ability Studies, 19,* 117–130.

Ivey, A. E., & Ivey, M. B. (1998). Reframing DSM-IV: Positive strategies from developmental counseling and therapy. *Journal of Counseling & Development, 76,* 334–350.

Jones, E. (1951). The problem of Paul Morphy: A contribution to the psychology of chess. In E. Jones (Ed.), *Essays in applied psycho-analysis, Vol I, Miscellaneous Essays* (pp. 165–196). London: The Hogarth Press.

Jung, C. G. (1968). *The archetypes and the collective unconscious* (The Collected Works of C. G. Jung, Bollingen Series XX Volume 9, Part 1). Princeton, NJ: Princeton University Press.

Kasparov, G. (with the participation of Plisetsky, D.) (2003). *On Fischer: My great predecessors, Part IV.* London: Gloucester.

Kazic, B. M. (1974). *International championship chess: A complete record of FIDE events.* London: Pitman.

Keene, R. (1990). *Chess: An illustrated history.* New York: Simon & Shuster.

Kendler, K. S., Czajkowski, N., Tambs, K., Torgersen, S., Aggen, S. H., Neale, M. C., & Reichborn-Kjennerud, T. (2006). Dimensional representations of *DSM-IV* cluster A personality disorders in a population-based sample of Norwegian twins: A multivariate study. *Psychological Medicine, 36I,* 1583–1591.

Kendler, K. S., Myers, J., Torgersen, S., Neale, M. C., & Reichborn-Kjennerud, T. (2007). The heritability of cluster A personality disorders assessed by both personal interview and questionnaire. *Psychological Medicine, 37,* 655–665.

Keri, S. (2009). Genes for psychosis and creativity: A promoter polymorphism of the neuregulin 1 gene is related to creativity in people with high intellectual achievement. *Psychological Science, 20,* 1070–1073.

Keri, S., Kiss, I., & Kelemen, O. (2009). Effects of a neuregulin 1 variant on conversion to schizophrenia and schizophreniform disorder in people at high risk for psychosis. *Molecular Psychiatry, 14,* 118–122.

Keri, S., Kiss, I., Seres, I., & Kelemen, O. (2008). A polymorphism of the neuregulin 1 gene [SNP8NRG243177/rs6994992] affects reactivity to expressed emotion in schizophrenia. *American Journal of Medical Genetics: Neuropsychiatric Genetics, 150,* 418–420.

Kessler, R. C., Berglund, P. A., Bruce, M. L., Koch, J. R., Laska, E. M., Leaf, P. J., Manderscheid, R. W., Rosenheck, R. A., Walters, E. E., & Wang, P. S. (2001). The prevalence and correlates of untreated serious mental illness. *Health Services Research, 36,* 987–1007.

Kessler, R. C., & Wang, P. S. (2008). The descriptive epidemiology of commonly occurring mental disorders in the United States. *Annual Review of Public Health, 29,* 115–129.

Kurtz, M. L. (1993). Paul Morphy: Louisiana's chess champion. *Louisiana History: The Journal of the Louisiana Historical Association, 34,* 175–199.

Lawson, D. (2010). *Paul Morphy: The pride and sorrow of chess.* (Edited by T. Aiello).

(Original published in 1976). Lafayette, LA: University of Louisiana at Lafayette Press.

Lopez, S. J., Edwards, L. M., Pedrotti, J. T., Prosser, E. C., LaRue, S., Spalitto, S. V., & Ulven, J. C. (2006). Beyond the *DSM-IV:* Assumptions, alternatives, and alterations. *Journal of Counseling & Development, 84,* 259–267.

Lukens, E., & Thorning, H. (2011). Siblings in families with mental illness. In J. Caspi (Ed.), *Sibling development: Implications for mental health practitioners* (pp. 195–219). New York: Springer.

Lyman, S. (2011). Documentary Interview from *Bobby Fischer against the world.* Documentary Film, executive producer Liz Garbus. New York: HBO Documentary Films.

McCall, S., Vilensky, J. A., Gilman, S., & Taubenberger, J, K. (2008). The relationship between encephalitis lethargic and influenza: A critical analysis. *Journal of Neurovirology, 14,* 177–185.

McClain, D. L. (2008). Players recall Fischer as inspiring and difficult. *New York Times,* January 19, p. B 10.

Mechanic, D., Bilder, S., & McAlpine, D. D. (2002). Employing persons with serious mental illness. *Health Affairs, 21,* 242–253.

Mental Health and Delusional Disorder Guide, WebMD, 2010. (http://www.webmd .com/schizophrenia/guide/delusional-disorder).

Millon, T., Grossman, S., Millon, C., Meagher, S., & Ramnath, R. (2004). *Personality disorders in modern life* (2nd ed.). New York: Wiley.

Morphy-Voitier, R. (1926). *Life of Paul Morphy in the Vieux Carre of New Orleans and abroad.* New Orleans: Privately oriented.

Morrison, J. (2007). *Diagnosis made easier: Principles and techniques for mental health clinicians.* New York: Guilford.

Morrison, J. (2006). *DSM-IV made easy: The clinician's guide to diagnosis.* New York: Guilford.

Moul, C. C., & Nye, J. V. C. (2009). Did the Soviets collude? A statistical analysis of championship chess 1940–1978. *Journal of Economic Behavior & Organization, 70,* 10–21.

Nabokov, V. (1964). *The Luzhin Defense.* New York: Penguin Classis (translated by Michael Scammell in collaboration with Vladimir Nabokov).

Nack, W. (2008). Checkered genius: His chess mastery is but one element of Bobby Fischer's curious legacy. *SI (Sports Illustrated) Vault, January 28.*

Narrow, W. E., Rae, D. S., Robins, L. N., & Regier, D. A. (2002). Revised prevalence estimates of mental disorders in the United States: Using a clinical significance criterion to reconcile 2 surveys' estimates. *Archives of General Psychiatry, 59,* 115–123.

Nicholas, P. (2002). Captured memories thirty years after the legendary Fischer-Spassky match, chess expert Shelby Lyman reminisces about his 15 minutes of fame as the TV commentator who put pawns in the parlor. *Philadelphia Inquirer, September 12,* p. D1.

Nicholas, P. (2009). Chasing the king of chess. *Los Angeles Times, September 21.*

Nicholas, P., & Benson, C. (2002). Files reveal how FBI hounded chess king.

Philadelphia Inquirer, November 17, p. A1.

Nicholas, P., & Benson, C. (2003). Life is not a board game. *The Philadelphia Inquirer, February 8.*

O'Donohue, W., Fowler, K. A., & Lilienfeld, S. O. (2007). *Personality disorders: Toward the DSM-V.* Los Angeles, CA: Sage.

O'Fee, J. (2008). *Chess and madness Part 3.* http//ww.impalapublications.com, October 15.

Penney, D., & Stastny, P. (2008). *The lives they left behind: Suitcases from a state hospital attic.* New York: Bellevue Literary Press.

Philipson, R. (1989). Chess and sex in le devoir du violence. *Callaloo, 38* (Winter), pp. 216–232.

Pierogy, J. (2010). *The five craziest and most brilliant chess grandmasters of all time.* http://amog.com/entertainment/celebrity/caraziest-brilliant-chess-grandmasters-time/.

Pies, R. (2007). How "objective" are psychiatric diagnoses? (Guess again). *Psychiatry, 4*(10), 18–22.

Polanczyk, G. V., Eizirik, M., Aranovich, V., Denardin, D., da Silva, T. L., da Conceicao, T. V., Pianca, T. G., & Rohde, L. A. (2003). Interrater agreement for the schedule for affective disorders and schizophrenia epidemiological version for school-age children (K-SADS-E). *Rev Bras Psiquiatr, 25,* 87–90.

Polgar, S. (with Truong, P.). (2005). *Breaking through: How the Polgar sisters changed the game of chess.* London: Gloucester.

Ponterotto, J. G. (2010). Multicultural personality: An evolving theory of optimal functioning in culturally heterogeneous societies. *The Counseling Psychologist, 38,* 714–758.

Ponterotto, J. G. (January/February, 2011). A psychological autopsy of Bobby Fischer. Research Essay in *Miller-McCune Magazine,* pp. 34–40.

Ponterotto, J. G., Casas, J. M., Suzuki, L. A., & Alexander, C. M. (Eds.). (2010). *Handbook of multicultural counseling* (3rd ed.). Los Angeles, CA: Sage.

Ponterotto, J. G., Utsey, S. O., & Pedersen, P. B. (2006). *Preventing prejudice: A guide for counselors, educators, and parents* (2nd ed.). Los Angeles, CA: Sage.

Quinn, B., & Hamilton, A. (2008). Bobby Fischer, chess genius, heartless son. *Timesonline, January 28, 2008* (http://www.timesonline.co.uk).

Regier, D. A., Narrow, W. E., Rae, D. S., Mandersheid, R. W., Locke, B. Z., & Goodwin, F. K. (1993). The de facto US mental and addictive disorders service system. Epidemiologic catchment area prospective 1-year prevalence rates of disorders and services. *Archives of General Psychiatry, 50,* 85–94.

Roring, R. W., & Charness, N. (2007). A multilevel model analysis of expertise in chess across the lifespan. *Psychology and Aging, 22,* 291–299.

Rothstein, E. (2008). Fischer versus the world: A chess giant's endgame. *The New York Times, January 19,* pp. B1, 9–10.

Runyan, W. M. (1982). *Life histories and psychobiography: Explorations in theory and method.* New York: Oxford University Press.

Saidy, A. (1992). *The battle of chess ideas.* Dallas, TX: Chess Digest Inc.

Saidy. A. (1994). *The march of chess ideas: How the century's greatest players have waged the war over chess strategy.* New York: Random House.

Saidy, A. (2004). Documentary Interview from *Anything to win: The mad genius of Bobby Fischer.* Documentary Film, executive producers Stephen Land, Geoffrey Prouid, & Peter Tarshis. New York: Jupiter Entertainment for A&E Television Network and Biography Channel.

Saidy, A. (2008). *Book Review of R. Fine's Bobby Fischer's conquest of the world's championship: The psychology and tactics of the title match* (pp. 11–14). New York: Ishi Press (First printed in 1973, David McKay.)

Saidy, A. (2011). Documentary Interview from *Bobby Fischer against the world.* Documentary Film, executive producer Liz Garbus. New York: HBO Documentary Films.

Saidy, A., & Lessing, N. (1974). *The world of chess.* New York: Random House.

Schultz, W. T. (Ed.). (2005a). *Handbook of psychobiography.* Oxford: Oxford University Press.

Schultz, W. T. (2005b). Introducing psychobiography. In W. T. Schultz's (Ed.), *Handbook of psychobiography* (pp. 3–18). Oxford: Oxford University Press.

Schultz, W. T. (2009). The psychological consequences of fame. *Psychology Today.* March 26: http://www.psychologytoday.com.

Schultz, W. T. (2011). *Tiny terror: Why Truman Capote (almost) wrote answered prayers.* Oxford: Oxford University Press.

Seirawan, Y. (2010). *Chess duels: My games with the world champions.* London: Gloucester.

Sergeant, P. W. (1957). *Morphy's games of chess.* New York: Dover.

Shedler, J. (2009). *Guide to SWAP-200 Interpretation.* Shedler-Westen Assessment Procedure: Where Science Meets Practice. www.SWAPassessment.org.

Shenk. D. (2006). *The immortal game: A history of chess.* New York: Doubleday.

Shneidman, E. S. (1969). Suicide, lethality, and the psychological autopsy. In E. S. Shneidman & M. Ortega (Eds.), *Aspects of depression* (pp. 225–250). Boston: Little, Brown.

Shneidman, E. S. (1973). *Deaths of man.* New York: Quadrangle Books.

Shneidman, E. S. (1981). The psychological autopsy. *Suicide & Life Threatening Behavior, 11,* 315–340.

Shneidman, E. S., & Farberow, N. L. (1961). Sample investigations of equivocal deaths. In N. L. Farberow & E. S. Shneidman (Eds.), *The cry for help* (pp. 118–129). New York: McGraw-Hill.

Sicher, F., Targ, E., Moore, D., & Smith, H. S. (1998). A randomized double-blind study of the effect of distant healing in a population with advanced AIDS: Report of a small scale study. *Western Journal of Medicine, 169,* 356–363.

Sneider, H. (2011). Documentary Interview from *Bobby Fischer against the world.* Documentary Film, executive producer Liz Garbus. New York: HBO Documentary Films.

Solotaroff, I. (1992). Bobby Fischer's endgame: Inside the crazy, secretive realm of the chess king who wants to keep the world in check. *Esquire Magazine* (December).

Spens, W. C. (1882). The pride and sorrow of chess. A five-stanza sonnet. *The Glasgow Weekly Herald,* November 25.

Suzuki, L. A., & Ponterotto, J. G. (Eds.). (2008). *Handbook of multicultural assessment: Clinical, psychological, and educational applications* (3rd ed.). San Francisco: Jossey-Bass (A Wiley imprint).

Taimanov, M. (2011). *Chessbase interview with Mark Taimanov. Going strong at 85–Mark Taimanov's birthday.* http://chessbase.com. February 16.

Targ, N. (Ed.). (2000). *Stories my grandmother wrote: Regina Wender Pustan, M.D., 1913–1997.* Unpublished manuscript.

Targ, R. (2008). *Do you see what I see: Memoirs of a blind biker–Lasers and love, ESP and the CIA, and the meaning of life.* www.hrpub.com: Hampton Roads.

The WHO World Mental Health Survey Consortium. (2004). Prevalence, severity, and unmet need for treatment of mental disorders in the world health organization world mental health surveys. *Journal of the American Medical Association, 291,* 2581–2590.

Truesdell, C. A. (1952). Paul Felix Nemenyi: 1895–1952. (Obituary). *Science, 116*(3009), 215–216.

Turkat, I. D. (1990). *The personality disorders.* New York: Pergamon.

U.S. Department of Health and Human Services. (2009). *Results from the 2009 National Survey on Drug Use and Health: Mental Health Findings.* Substance Abuse and Mental Health Services Administration Office of Applied Studies.

Vollstadt-Klein, S., Grimm, O., Kirsch, P., & Bilalic, M. (2010). Personality of elite male and female chess players and its relation to chess skill. *Learning and Individual Differences, 20,* 517–521.

Waitzkin, F. (1988). *Searching for Bobby Fischer: The world of chess, observed by the father of a child prodigy.* New York: Random House.

Wall, B. (2006). *Robert James (Bobby) Fischer.* www.geocites.com.

Way, B. B., Allen, M. H., Mumpower, J. L., Stewart, T. R., & Banks, S. M. (1998). Interrater agreement among psychiatrists in psychiatric emergency assessment. *American Journal of Psychiatry, 155,* 1423–1428.

Weber, B. (2008). Bobby Fischer, troubled genius of chess, is dead. *The New York Times, January 19,* pp. A1, A16.

Yalom, M. (2004). *Birth of the chess queen: A history.* New York: HarperCollins.

Zalaquett, C. P., Fuerth, K. M., Stein, C., Ivey, A. E., & Ivey, M. B. (2008). Reframing the DSM-IV-TR from a multicultural/social justice perspective. *Journal of Counseling & Development, 86,* 364–371.

Zimmerman, M. (1994). Diagnosing personality disorders. *Archives of General Psychiatry, 51,* 225–245.

Zuckerman, M. (1999). *Vulnerability to psychopathology: A biosocial model.* Washington, DC: American Psychological Association.

NAME INDEX

SUBJECT INDEX

ABOUT THE AUTHOR

Joseph G. Ponterotto, Ph.D., is a Professor of Counseling Psychology and Coordinator of the Mental Health Counseling Program in Fordham University's Graduate School of Education, Lincoln Center (Manhattan) Campus. Prior to arriving at Fordham University in 1987, he was a member of the counseling psychology faculty at the University of Nebraska, in Lincoln, Nebraska. He received his M.A. (1981) and Ph.D. (1985) in Counseling Psychology at the University of California at Santa Barbara (UCSB).

Dr. Ponterotto's primary teaching and research interests are in the area of multicultural counseling, quantitative and qualitative research methods, career counseling and assessment, and clinical practice. He is both a licensed psychologist and mental health counselor in the state of New York. Dr. Ponterotto maintains a small private practice in New York City where he works with a broad array of culturally diverse clients, a number of whom are chess players. His clinical specialty is on the intersection of personal development, career development, and quality of life within a sociocultural context.

Dr. Ponterotto is the co-author or co-editor of a number of previous books including the *Handbook of Multicultural Counseling* (Sage Publications), the *Handbook of Multicultural Assessment: Clinical, Psychological, and Educational Applications* (Wiley & Sons), P*reventing Prejudice: A Guide for Counselors, Educators, and Parents* (Sage Publications), and the *Handbook of Racial/Ethnic Minority Counseling Research* (Charles C Thomas, Publisher, Ltd.). An active researcher, Dr. Ponterotto has authored or co-authored roughly 95 peer-reviewed journal articles in counseling and psychology. In 1994, he was the co-winner of the "Early Career Scientist/Practitioner" Award of the Division of Counseling Psychology within the American Psychological Association (APA). In 2007 he received the Janet E. Helms Award for Mentoring and Scholarship awarded by Teachers College of Columbia University, one of the multicultural psychology field's most distinguished honors. He is a Fellow of the American Psychological Association and the former Associate Editor of the *Journal of Counseling Psychology*. He is an avid chess enthusiast and has been playing chess and following the life of Bobby Fischer since the early 1970s.

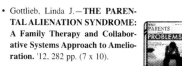
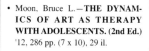
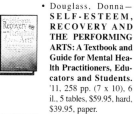